FERNAND LÉGER

F. LÉGER

by GASTON DIEHL

CROWN PUBLISHERS

Title page: SELF-PORTRAIT, 1930
Drawing
Musée National Fernand Léger,
Biot, France

Translated from the French by:
ALICE SACHS AND A. CLARKE

Collection published under the direction of:
MADELEINE LEDIVELEC-GLOECKNER

Library of Congress Cataloging in Publication Data

Diehl, Gaston.
    Fernand Léger.

    1. Léger, Fernand, 1881–1955.   2. Painters–France–
Biography. I. Title.
ND553.L58D53   1985   759.4 [B]   81–19604
ISBN: 0–517–547112   AACR2

PHOTOGRAPHS

OLIVER BAKER, New York – PHOTOS CAUVIN, Paris – GEOFFREY CLEMENTS,
New York – COLORPHOTO H. HINZ, Basel – JACQUELINE HYDE, Paris – IFOT,
Grenoble – BRUCE JONES, Centerport – ROBERT E. MATES AND MARY DOULON,
New York – JACQUES MER, Antibes – OTTO E. NELSON, New York – SERVICE
PHOTOGRAPHIQUE DU MUSÉE NATIONAL D'ART MODERNE, Paris – DUANE
SUTER, Baltimore – JOHN WEBB, CHEAM, Surrey

PRINTED IN ITALY – INDUSTRIE GRAFICHE CATTANEO S.P.A., BERGAMO

The artist still perseveres although misunderstood

There are many among those of us who were friends of his who feel that Fernand Léger disappeared from the scene too early when he died in 1955. Fate struck him down brutally just as he was beginning, during his last years, to fulfill the aspirations that he had nurtured for so long and to receive commissions from every part of the world for the monumental artistic creations he had always hoped to work on. If, like Picasso, he had only lived for another twenty years, how many more murals might there have been to enrich still further the abundant legacy which he left us and to raise his reputation to the heights which he deserved!

However, we should not complain: we should be grateful for his many accomplishments. Thanks to Nadia Léger and Georges Bauquier, the museums at Biot and Lisores have been completed and soon will be followed by that at Gif-sur-Yvette. Thus the artist's work will be within everyone's grasp. Although his name will henceforth be well known and included in all the textbooks, his art is still not fully appreciated. This was demonstrated by the recent retrospective at the Grand Palais in Paris.

Lack of acceptance by the man in the street, of which Léger complained bitterly on several occasions, has still not been overcome entirely. Even his friends and most fervent supporters did not hesitate to express doubts and reservations about his ability to win a wide following and exert a powerful influence. Franck Elgar wrote: "For a long while, because he was so thoroughly a child of his time and was never willing to divorce himself from the period in which he lived, his own era refused to accord him his rightful place in the artistic world. He, who more than anyone else put his stamp on the period, was the last person to have his contribution recognized." In the same vein André Verdet observed: "The modern age, which Fernand Léger heralded and embraced through his art, both in his murals and in his easel paintings, has probably not yet fully grasped the importance of his work and of its penetrating qualities."

Why was he ostracized? Why this rejection by a society whose aesthetic concepts he so largely helped forge? What is the explanation for the obvious failure to appreciate the importance of his contribution, which, as we shall see later, he defined very early on in all clarity and subsequently developed in a spirit of strict unity?

Perhaps the artist himself occasionally displayed a tendency to overemphasize a rough style—an ingenuous character of popular imagery that in the long run disappointed and bewildered the public. He simultaneously made enemies of those who, much to his regret, were not able to understand what he was trying to do and of collectors, who did not always support him as he might have wished. As early as 1913–14, he anticipated with remarkable clairvoyance a future dominated by the machine, by the urban environment, and by materialism. Perhaps this was premature if we consider that it is only today that we have started to devote attention to these major problems in relation to both their artistic and human implications.

In this brief analysis of Léger's aims and the rich diversity of his activities, a primary objective will be to clear up these misunderstandings and to ascertain how much responsibility for them can be ascribed to individuals or groups, or, as Léger claimed, to society as a whole; in this way we might then be able to bridge the gulf of incomprehensibility that has existed far too long about some of the most significant works of our time.

A precocious maturity develops in solitude

Despite his jovial good nature, his air of a "husky banterer" in the popular mold, his informality and, later, his social and political involvement, which invariably assured him friendly relations with those around him, Fernand Léger displayed an undeniable fondness for solitude throughout his life.

Born in Argentan, France, in 1881 to a father who was a livestock farmer—his father died shortly afterward—and to a mother whom he adored, Léger soon came to feel alone with his dream of becoming an artist. Then, at the age of sixteen, having finished his studies at the local school and at a Catholic school at Tinchebray, he took the advice of an uncle

STUDY FOR THREE
PORTRAITS, 1910–11
Oil on canvas
76 3/4″ × 45 7/8″
(195 × 116.5 cm)
Milwaukee Art Center

SMOKE OVER ROOFTOPS, 1911
Oil on canvas   21 3/4″ × 18 1/2″ (55 × 47 cm) Staatliche Kunsthalle, Karlsruhe, Germany

and from 1897 to 1899 studied architecture at Caen. Afterward he worked as a draftsman for an architect in Paris for three years. He completed his military service at Versailles in the Second Corps of Engineers and was finally able to satisfy his aspirations.

In 1903 he was once again alone, whether at the École des Arts Décoratifs or at the École des Beaux-Arts, in the classes given by Léon Gérôme, an understanding teacher (his classes were open to the general public), and with Gabriel Ferrier at the Académie Julian and even in visits to the Louvre. He shared a studio with André Mare, also a native of Argentan, in the Rue Saint Placide and then on the Avenue du Maine. He led a hard life, working in turn as a draftsman for an architect and as a photographer's retoucher. The admiration that he felt for Henri Martin at the time is revealed in his first pictures, painted in 1905, such as *My Mother's Garden, Portrait of the Artist's Uncle,* with its vigorous strokes and thick texture, and even more in the *Portrait of Blasini,* painted in 1907 in Corsica. Léger went to Corsica several times, staying with his friend Viel, in an attempt to restore his failing health. Whether he was affected by the stimulating and colorful atmosphere of the island, as Matisse had been, or simply by the memory of visits he had probably made to the Salon d'Automne and the Salon des Indépendants, he introduced certain elements of Fauvism into his *Self-Portrait* and into the landscapes which he painted while there, such as *Corsican Village: Sunset,* and which revealed Cézanne's influence. This was also apparent in *The Bathers,* a work which has since disappeared, but traces of it can be found in the memoirs of Gleizes, a French Cubist painter.

Léger returned to Paris for good in 1908 and at long last he found an artistic climate in which his work could flourish. He settled in the Danzig Arcade in La Ruche, which sheltered a whole commune of artists such as Laurens, Lipchitz, and Archipenko, who gave him some very useful advice, and later Chagall, Soutine, and in particular Delaunay, who became his friend. Some writers living in the vicinity also went there, including Reverdy, Max Jacob, Apollinaire, Maurice Raynal, who was to be one of the first to review his work, and Blaise Cendrars, who subsequently became his most faithful friend. Léger, full of enthusiasm at that time, did not hesitate to send his paintings of Corsica to the Salon d'Automne of 1908 and 1909 and his drawings in 1910.

Yet he was again a loner when, in 1909, he launched into the Cubist venture, supported only by the admiration which he felt for Cézanne, whose famous 1907 retrospective had led to such a profound change among the new generation. The crisis which Léger went through at this time was so great that, as he himself admitted, he destroyed almost all his old paintings. His new experiments were fumbling—*The Seamstress,* for example, stressing mass and bulk in a manner also adopted by La Fresnaye. Even more illustrative is *Table and Fruit;* its style is closer to the contemporary concepts of orthodox Cubism. It attracted Kahnweiler's attention, who in 1910 opened the doors of his gallery on the Rue Vignon to the artist.

Early that same year, Léger had developed sufficient confidence to submit for the first time five works to the Salon des Indépendants: one reclining woman, two still lifes, and two sketches. Also, he began to paint a series of contrasting forms that he would develop in depth, as is illustrated by the small picture *Smoke over Rooftops,*[1] which he gave to André Mare's young wife as a wedding present. Above all, he started work on a major painting

1) See p. 8

9

that would take close to two years to complete and was to be the chief attraction at the next Salon. This was *Nudes in a Landscape,* later to be called *Nudes in the Forest.*[1] In his memoirs Gleizes jokingly relates how, thanks to Alexandre Mercereau, he was already associated with Metzinger, Le Fauconnier, and Delaunay; he welcomed Léger to his team and at "La Closerie," with some friends, the poets Apollinaire, Salmon, and Allard, drew up a plan to tamper with the elections to the Salon des Indépendants. In this way he hoped to be free to organize, along with Marie Laurencin, Room 41, which was to become the Mecca of Cubism and earned them, according to Gleizes, overnight fame. We are well aware that Gleizes was somewhat inclined to take all the credit for himself and, in the absence of leading actors such as Picasso and Braque, to assign himself the role of head of the new movement, whose laws he and Metzinger promulgated in a work which appeared the following year.

Léger's work played a starring role as much because of its huge dimensions as on account of its original appearance. The pun linking "Cubist" and "Tubist" went from mouth to mouth and became the joke of the day. His own companions made no attempt to hide their perplexity at the absence of any reference to the accepted rules of Cubism. Before Apollinaire subsequently penned the poetic description in which he evokes ". . . that deep greenish light which comes down from the leaves," in his review of April 11, 1911, he referred prosaically to a "cylindrical painting" and the "barbaric appearance of a pile of tires." Metzinger, in his article in the "Journal de Paris," was more favorably inclined. Nevertheless, while justifiably noting the effect of chiaroscuro, he strained to discover other influences. "Fernand Léger measures the day and the night, weighs blocks, calculates resistance factors. His composition. . . is a living body; the trees and the figures are its organs. An austere painter, Léger is passionately interested in the profound aspect of painting which reaches out to the biological sciences and was foreshadowed by Michelangelo and Leonardo." Although the comment was belated, Gleizes did indulge in some unsympathetic irony, saying that "Mass and bulk were treated in the same way as shaded areas are handled in architecture of mechanical models."

Let us rather refer to the article written by Léger for Kahnweiler in 1919, which attempted to justify a position that owed nothing to Cubism:

> I was exhibiting *Nudes in the Forest* at the Salon des Indépendants. It showed the influence of David and Rousseau, being a reaction against the diffused light of neo-Impressionism. An obsession with volumes and shapes which is at the root of my work. . . I carried the period of reaction as far as I could, dislocating forms and neglecting color. When I mastered my form (molded volume), then color reappeared. At first it was gray, reminiscent of Cézanne; then, little by little, it gained in importance. In short, I reacted against Impressionism not because of its excessive use of color but because it lacked constructive force. I believe I am clearly in the line of the French Impressionists. My paintings, like theirs, will always tend to be dynamic. I have never been good at combining surfaces in the way that is an essential characteristic of Cubism. My compositions are made of masses in colorful movement, each one considered as a whole. To accentuate the movements, I use the contrast between soft and hard forms, whether I am painting smoke or women.

1) See p. 5

THE WEDDING, *c.* 1910–11
Oil on canvas   101 1/8″ × 81″ (257 × 206 cm)
Musée National d'Art Moderne, CNAC Georges Pompidou, Paris

This painting is felt to be most important to the artist's future, in spite of some visible deficiencies as far as the rhythm is concerned, and still more in the case of the color. I would be tempted to compare it to Paolo Ucello's *Battle* in its use of multiple perspectives, its skillfully intertwined masses, and its powerful feeling. At the end of his life, Léger still felt inspired by Ucello when he confessed to Verdet: "What a teacher. . . I am studying him in detail. . . He puts into practice the vital law of contrasts. . . This Paolo Ucello knew how to paint machinery before I did."

This first important work by Léger contains the seeds of almost all the elements that he was eventually to use, such as deformed, webbed hands, cone-shaped torsos resembling fragments of machinery, dislocated masses, and so forth. It clearly indicates his determination to open up a path for himself, impelled by the most intense dynamism, of which he was to be the sole pioneer, with the possible exception of Marcel Duchamp and Jacques Villon, whose experiments with movement were closer to Futurism than to Cubism. He would have occasion to explain his own thoughts on this subject in lectures he gave shortly afterward, the only one in his group of artists to attempt such an explanation.

During 1911, Léger who was at the time living in a small apartment at 13 Rue de l'Ancienne Comédie, stepped up the work he put on exhibition: in Brussels, at the eighth exhibition of the Indépendants with his Parisian friends of the Salon des Indépendants; in Paris, at the second exhibition of the Société Normande de Peinture Moderne in the Rue Tronchet. Even more important, he made a twofold contribution to the Salon d'Automne. The first was *Study for Three Portraits*,[1] an interesting work that was subsequently exhibited at the Armory Show in the United States in 1913 and found a permanent home in the Milwaukee Art Center; the other—a notable fact which Delevoy was the first to stress—was the designs for a dining room and a study drawn up with his friends La Fresnaye, Duchamp, Villon, and Rouault, to be executed by André Mare. They clearly illustrate how early in his career Léger revealed his ambitions in this field.

Once again we quote Apollinaire, who showed his enthusiasm for Room 8 of the Cubists at the Salon d'Automne, calling it "the greatest achievement in contemporary French art," but remained cautious in his judgment of Léger, whom he saw as "still searching for a style." In an article he wrote for "Bandeau d'Or," Gleizes was more perceptive: "The firm resolve to achieve only a sculptural effect gives his compositions an aspect which at first is slightly disquieting. But the longer one looks at the painting, the more one understands it, the more the motif is revealed, the more it rises, becomes intensely alive, under the impetus of a curious but very real dynamism."

Study for Three Portraits is a very attractive painting, delicate in color, but enlivened by a strong upward rhythm that bursts upon the senses, a work that its creator modestly called a tentative experiment. It marked a turning point, and was, a few months later, to lead to the more ambitious and spectacular work that he carefully prepared for the forthcoming Salon des Indépendants, *The Wedding*[2] or *Composition with Figures*. More accomplished than *Study for Three Portraits, Composition with Figures* is a masterpiece with its vast size, its stronger colors, and its quick succession of rhythms. Human figures, more numerous than in *Study for Three Portraits,* are arranged and intertwined in light, fragmentary masses within a space that is divided into vertical strips accentuated by alternating

1) See p. 7
2) See p. 11

NUDE MODEL IN THE STUDIO, 1912–13
Oil on burlap   50 3/8″ × 37 5/8″ (127.8 × 95.7 cm) The Solomon R. Guggenheim Museum, New York

CONTRASTING FORMS, 1913. Oil on canvas. Acquavella Galleries, New York

JULY 14, 1914
Oil on canvas   28 3/4″ × 23 1/2″ (73 × 60 cm) Musée National Fernand Léger, Biot, France

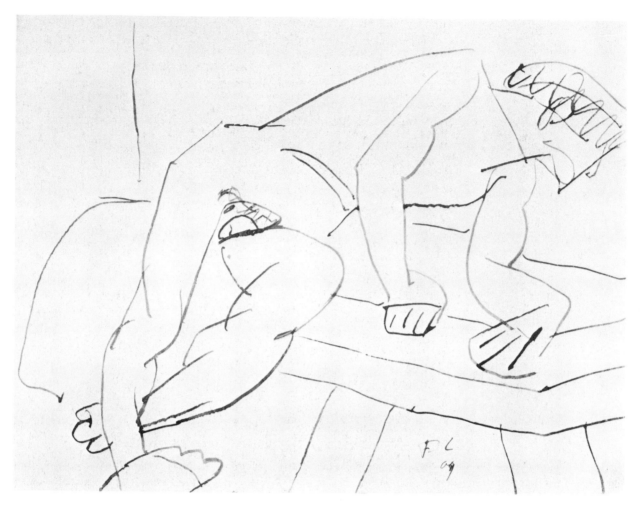

Nude Figure, 1909
Pen drawing   9 3/4" × 13 3/8" (25 × 34 cm)
Louise Leiris Gallery, Paris

Woman in Red and Green, 1914
Oil on canvas   39 3/8" × 31 7/8" (100 × 81 cm)
Musée National d'Art Moderne
CNAC Georges Pompidou, Paris

geometric forms. It seems to be at the same time a summing-up and a farewell. As can be seen from previous drawings and paintings done between 1908 and 1910, Léger had already examined the possibilities of such dislocation of forms. Delaunay had also used the device in his series *The Eiffel Tower* and soon afterward Chagall followed suit. Léger wanted to go beyond this, to bring out and clarify the contrasts between masses. In this sense *The Smokers* (Solomon Guggenheim Museum, New York), though it was painted at the same time as *Study for Three Portraits,* already shows a different orientation. Trees, houses, and clouds are in clear contrast in the series of paintings from 1912, such as *Smoke over Rooftops.* In passing, it should be noted that Léger was a close friend of the Duchamp family in Puteaux; together, they exchanged ideas about such problems as speed, movement, and composition. The two Duchamp brothers used curvilinear and contrasting rhythms—Marcel Duchamp in his *Portrait of Chess Players,* dated 1911, and Jacques Villon in *Smoke and Trees in Blossom,* painted in 1912.

I am convinced that Léger also intended to put an end to his ambiguous relationship with Cubism. Through chance it was assumed in the Salons that he owed allegiance to the so-called Cubists. Yet he did not agree with their principles and really belonged more to Montparnasse, where he had always lived, than to Montmartre. He became acquainted with the leaders of the Cubist movement, Picasso and Braque, only belatedly, through Apollinaire. At no time did he consider following them in their experiments. In spite of this, he did not remain indifferent to the results which they achieved, and in *The Wedding,* faithful to the lesson learned from Cézanne, he resorted to bluish or golden-gray tones and multiplied at will the intersections of planes and lines. This led Apollinaire to describe the picture as "an unfinished work which can have an impact only on knowledgeable minds." Subsequently, Léger was usually satisfied to give the Cubists a conspiratorial wink in the corner of a picture in one form or another, such as a few block letters in *Nude Model in the Studio,*[1] a prismatic vase on a stool in *Reclining Woman,*[2] or a multifaceted glass on the corner of a table in *Woman in Blue*—which was intended for the 1912 Salon d'Automne—and in *Still Life with Book,* which he finished in 1913. These morsels of testimony might equally well be interpreted as expressions of his lasting desire to remain faithful to the concept of visual realism, which he defended so strongly, unlike the Cubists, who, in his opinion, advocated the opposing tenets of conceptual realism. Moreover, in October 1912 and in the following year he participated in the Section d'Or exhibition, sponsored by Apollinaire and financed by Picabia, which attempted to throw off the yoke of Cubism, in spite of the presence of Gleizes, Metzinger, Gris, and Marcoussis, alongside the founders Jacques Villon and Marcel Duchamp, assisted by La Fresnaye, Valensim and Dumont.

Full of enthusiasm, that same year he exhibited in Paris at the June Salon of the Société Normande de Peinture Moderne, in Moscow at the "Jack of Diamonds" exhibition organized by Malevich, and in Amsterdam at the Modern Kunst Kring. Even more notable, for the first time he showed a small collection of his works at Kahnweiler's, who signed a contract with him in October 1913.

He proclaimed his need for independence by a clear emphasis on harmony in *Woman in Blue,* perhaps more forcefully in the first, very simple version (now in the Biot Museum)

1) See p. 13
2) See p. 45

18

than in the second version, which was fuller, more detailed, and more elaborate and which he showed in the Salon d'Automne. As he explained later, "The Cézannian nuances were finished with by 1912. I shall not revert to them. My colors are lively. I went to that point, to the abstract, in order to break away from Cézanne." He was more precise later on: "I should like to achieve colors which stand out on their own, a red which is very red, a blue which is very blue. Delaunay was inclined to use subtle shades, while I openly tended to utilize strong colors and masses. . . In 1912, I discovered the virtue of pure color circumscribed by geometrical forms."

Over and above this experiment, which satisfied him only partially, Léger remained firm in his decision to pursue a solitary course, rejecting both the "spider's web" painting of the Cubists, as he sarcastically called it and avoiding excessive abstractionism, which at the time was attracting several of his companions, led by Delaunay. His principal concern, in line with a theory that was uniquely his and that, moreover, he was about to proclaim publicly, was to bring about a synthesis and to combine the visual realism of the Impressionists and the conceptual realism that is in vogue today. The inclusion of color obliged him partly to abandon chiaroscuro and the gradation of light and shade and to seek new solutions to suggest mass, a problem that continued to obsess him. If the furious experimentation in which he engaged during 1913 and 1914 sometimes led him to reflect the teaching of Cézanne in the treatment of some of his themes, he was nevertheless removing himself gradually from that artist's influence. It was not so much that Léger doubted his previous convictions or took a step backward; rather, he consciously expanded the kinds of subjects he wished to handle and the means of expressing them artistically, reassessing these two facets of his work after mature reflection. The obvious harmony and joyous spirit with which the numerous works dating from that time are infused caused René Déroudille to describe it, with perfect justification, as the great "period of contrasts."

Successively, and with infinitesimal variations, he painted on the theme of *Contrasting Forms,*[1] still in the realm of the abstract, and, at the other end of the spectrum, the human figure, as in *The Alarm Clock,* or simply views of nature, as in *House under the Trees.* Perhaps he chose one of the latter to exhibit at the 1913 Salon des Indépendants—although it is not mentioned in the catalogue—for he finally won a compliment from Apollinaire, who wrote: "The painter must be given credit for showing a real *picture* for the first time. It is a very large and very serious work of art." The change in the poet's attitude toward Léger was striking; he even went so far as to include him in the book devoted to Cubist painters that he was bringing out at the time and to describe his work in flattering lyrical terms. This was still true at the beginning of 1914, when he took up previous themes again, as in *Woman in Red and Green*[2] and *House under the Trees,* or developed new ones, such as *The Balcony* and *The Stairway,*[3] which he attempted to perfect in three different versions, an experiment that paralleled but differed from that of Marcel Duchamp. All his paintings of that period remain closely akin and are animated by the same flashes of forceful dynamism, whatever the theme. In their black outlines, which emphasize and define their contours, the strong colors set in stripes alternating with white spaces—kinetic art

1) See p. 14
2) See p. 17
3) See p. 21

before it even had a name—and the extraordinary profusion of geometric forms—cubes, parallelepipeds, cylinders, cones, ovoids, almost all of them resemble machinery in motion, with revolving cranks and gears.

Although he tried to exclude any hint of sentimentality from his work, the masterful and resolute thrust of his paintings and their sense of abounding joy reflected his life at the time. The year 1913 was critical for him since, together with international and national recognition, it brought him spiritual and material security in the form of an exclusive contract with Kahnweiler, which enabled him to rent a studio at 86 Rue Notre-Dame-des-Champs, where he was to stay indefinitely. He participated in two of the outstanding events of the day: the Armory Show (with two paintings), which between February and May traveled to New York and Chicago and from there to Boston, and the First Salon d'Automne in Berlin (with nine paintings and some drawings). In France, concurrently with Apollinaire's above-mentioned book about Cubist painters, Roger Allard devoted an article in "Soirées de Paris" to him. Above all, in May he gave a lecture at the Académie Wassiliev on "The Origins of Painting and Its Representational Value" which was published in Paris in "Montjoie." Shortly afterward, it was reprinted in Berlin in "Der Sturm" (with one of his drawings on the cover) and in Bergen in "Kunst og Kultur," and reviewed in Florence by Umberto Boccioni in "Lacerba." He continued his analysis in May 1914 with "Contemporary Revelations in Painting," which "Soirées de Paris" published in its June issue.

Why both of these lectures had a worldwide impact—the second less so because of the outbreak of war—can be easily explained. For the first time an artist had candidly given his views on his problems and objectives and had examined his relationship to the time in which he lived, with greater clarity than Matisse had done previously.

He not unreasonably claimed to be in the line of Cézanne and the Impressionists, who "were the first to reject the notion that a subject had an absolute value and considered instead its relative value." He regarded the Impressionists as the "Primitives" of contemporary art, which was destined to develop their colored dynamism by using new techniques that "result in an intense realism." He recommended the use of "pictorial contrasts of colors, lines and shapes" in order to achieve the "conceptual realism" that dominates contemporary art. He advocated doing away with sentimentality and concerning oneself solely with the plastic composition of the painting. He therefore suggested a "concentration of techniques," a "composition with a multiplicity of contrasts." He used as an example the "visual effect of curved and rounded smoke rising between houses" and suggested grouping "the curves with the greatest possible variety" and "framing them in the hard, dry surfaces of the houses." He concluded: "Contrast = dissonance . . . consequently, contrast = maximum expressiveness." Already, he was exhorting painters and architects, issuing a recall to order, proclaiming a veritable profession of faith that would henceforth be his own. "I am convinced that we have reached a concept of art as vast as the greatest of the periods which preceded it: the same predilection for large works, the same effort, but the same collective participation." To make certain that painting and sculpture did not enter into competition, which he deemed foolish and futile, with color photography and cinematography, as well as novels and plays, he encouraged them "to limit themselves reasonably to their own goals." He optimistically announced the triumph of the modern concept, which "is not a passing abstraction . . . [but] the total expression of a new generation to whose needs it responds and whose aspirations it understands."

20

THE STAIRWAY, 1914
Oil on canvas
56 7/8″ × 36 3/4″
(144.5 × 93.5 cm)
Moderna Museet,
Stockholm

With unusual foresight (which he was the only one to exhibit), he demanded that the artist be "in tune with his time." He placed a firm emphasis on "the new visual state imposed by the evolution of means of transport, by their speed," feeling that railroads and automobiles "have monopolized dynamism." In this, his theories were close to those of the Futurists, but his analysis of the situation was different and more thorough. He underlined the need henceforth to take account of the notion of speed. He boldly defended billboards dotting the countryside, posters on walls, and illuminated signs; he invited artists to become involved in advertising in order to transform "the ancient garb of cities." He glorified the presence of "the yellow or red poster which roars out in the timid landscape" and judged it to be "the most beautiful new pictorial effect imaginable." Anticipating his own future, he invited each of his colleagues to "define the modern ambience," to seek inspiration by observing locomotives and automobiles and other kinds of machines as well as billboards, and "the most banal, the tritest of subjects—a nude woman in a studio." Later he would recall a visit with Marcel Duchamp and Brancusi to an aircraft exhibition and comment that he had been much more interested in the engines than in the propellers.

The world war that broke out suddenly suspended all activity, and on August 2, 1914, Léger was drafted into the army as a sapper. The brusque end to this period in his life compels us to conclude by asking whether it was necessary to spend so much time describing mere lectures and a period of initiation, which was followed by an interruption of his career. Probably in order to place his evolution up to that time in its proper context, in 1922, Léger himself said quite frankly: "Before the war there was no real decision; I fought outside influences, fought popular taste, displaying nothing but timidity and equivocation." We can answer with conviction that the beginnings of a great artist are always important and, as far as Léger is concerned, very important indeed.

The war, of course, was to sweep everything else aside, and afterward it would take him a while to regain the happy circumstances he had enjoyed before it. The dashing spirit that was so evident in *July 14, 1914,*[1] a painting that rang out like a clarion call, appeared subdued in the first works that he painted in 1917 during his convalescence in the hospital at Villepinte, such as *The Card Player,* a final and paradoxical tribute to Cézanne, and *Soldier with a Pipe,*[2] a dramatic return to the angular robot figures that belonged to an earlier period but were now appropriate to the dehumanized, mechanized universe surrounding them. Kahnweiler also disappeared for several years. His art collection was regarded as German property and confiscated by the French government, to be sold off at scandalously low prices in four successive auctions at the Hôtel Drouot between 1921 and 1923. In this way 204 of Léger's drawings and 36 of his paintings were thrown on the market. This was a major handicap to him, which he had great difficulty in overcoming, in spite of the support he received from Léonce Rosenberg, the art dealer. Léger himself had been gassed at the front at Verdun in September 1916 and underwent prolonged medical treatment before he was finally invalided out of the army at the end of 1917. Yet these events only accelerated the progress that he had begun to make; the evolution of his art proceeded according to plan, and he was to achieve in his work all the goals which, with amazing foresight, he had set himself.

1) See p. 15
2) See p. 29

22

The painful pause imposed by circumstances was in a sense a blessing, for it gave the artist an opportunity to search his soul and to rediscover a human, down-to-earth milieu far removed from the atmosphere of the studio; in short, to be in direct touch with reality. As far as possible, he drew from life the scenes in which he had been personally involved, the ordinary men whose harsh existence he shared *(Soldiers in a Dug-Out, Sappers at Work)*, and the equipment around him, such as field kitchens, cannons, and destroyed aircraft. Sometimes, during a halt, he even indulged himself in little oil studies, and he once made a collage on the covers of some ammunition crates *(The Card Players,*[1] *Horses in the Cantonment)*. He continued to employ his usual style, with its syncopated rhythms and its accumulation of strongly defined masses.

He revealed the consequences of this when, in 1922, he wrote: "Three years spent without touching a brush, but in contact with the rawest, most violent reality. As soon as I was demobilized, I benefited from those harsh years: I reached a decision and began to paint using pure tones, clearly defined colors and huge masses, making no concessions. I progressed beyond tidy, tasteful arrangements, muted grayish tones, and dead surfaces in the background. I stopped floundering; I saw things clearly. I am not afraid to say candidly that the war brought about my fulfillment."

During the first months of 1918 he seemed to be hurrying to make up for lost time, as if he wanted to exert an enormous effort in the last year of the war to exorcise his awful memories and compensate for the unproductive years. Like other artists who had returned from the trenches, such as Derain and Vlaminck, and even those who had not been drafted, such as Matisse and Picasso, and even more especially those who, like him, had paid a heavy price and suffered physically—men such as Braque and Cendrars—Léger was eager to smile at life once again. Unlike them, however, Léger was not about to cast even a fleeting glance at flowers, fruits, or female nudes. The machine remained the sole focus of his interest; he strove hard, with obvious pleasure and remarkable poetic feeling, to start from scratch, to imagine it in all its complexity and obsessiveness. For him a machine did not serve—as in the case of Picabia, Max Ernst, or Marcel Duchamp—as an outlet for irony, rebellion, or sexuality, but as a vehicle with which to express his admiration for the period. At the same time he kept his distance from Futurism, as is proved by his "Pensées," published in Rome in "Valori Plastici."

Thus, he entered the "Machine Age," for which he was to become the spokesman, briefly reviving the abstract assemblages of pre-1914, with their different geometric solids linked together in a rising movement but now lightened by subtle shaded colors, as in *Contrasting Forms,* or to arrange the rhythm better by slowing it down, as in *Propellers* and the illustrations that he did for Blaise Cendrars's book "I Have Killed." He immediately changed these compositions considerably by introducing the two themes that were to be of major significance in his work—human figures and the city. Initially, he evoked these themes, which truly mark his return to life, by scattering objects around the composition in the same way as he liked to dot the canvas with black letters, as in *The*

1) See p. 25

Nude Woman, 1910
Pen drawing   13" × 9 3/4" (33 × 25 cm)
Louise Leiris Gallery, Paris

Acrobats,[1] *The Mechanic in the Factory,*[2] *The Pink Tug,* and *The Circus.*[3] Finally *Discs*[4] is a work that was important by dint of its size and its qualities. He used Delaunay's principles of composition almost as if these provided him with an excuse, and boldly tackled flat pure tints that he put together like skillfully contrived mechanism of a clock so as to "succeed in giving an impression of forcefulness and power," as he said later.

He was encouraged by this prelude to happy fulfillment, and in 1919, on the return of peace, he once again took up all his former activities. In February he exhibited at Léonce Rosenberg's Galerie de l'Effort Moderne, then in Antwerp at the Galerie Sélection, and once again illustrated a book by Cendrars in which he shows how much he was attracted to the cinema and to the use of huge block letters in color in a picture such as *The End of the World Filmed by the Angel of Our Lady.* He started to experiment and to head in new directions, as revealed in *Abstract Composition,* which was already a Purist work, and in *Men in the City,*[5] which demonstrated a new sense of composition. But his chief efforts, after numerous sketches and tentative drafts, were devoted to a manifesto in the form of a large painting, *The City,*[6] a procedure not unusual for him, which was intended for the forthcoming Salon des Indépendants of 1920. He did not hesitate to show it prior to the Salon at the International Exhibition at Geneva. As he was to explain in describing the far-reaching scope of this act:

I made use solely of pure, flat tints in the picture. Technically, the work represents an artistic revolution. Without chiaroscuro or modulations it has been possible to

1) See p. 32
2) See p. 27
3) See p. 30
4) See p. 31
5) See p. 37
6) See p. 35

THE CARD PLAYERS, 1915
Oil and paper
on wood panel
15 3/8″ × 10 1/4″
(39 × 26 cm)
Collection: Mr. and
Mrs. Israel Rosen,
Baltimore, Maryland

produce depth and movement. The advertising business was the first to take advantage of what this has to offer. The pure tone of the blues, red, and yellows actually leaps out of the canvas and imprints itself on posters, in shop windows, on roadsides and on traffic signs. Color has become free. It is now reality, an entity unto itself.

At the 1920 Salon, Léger also showed a painting that he had just finished. It was somewhat smaller than *The City,* and, as is indicated by the title, *Discs in the City,* he achieved a synthesis of his two previous efforts. He revealed a similar kaleidoscope of cut-up planes that fitted into one another and were moved by a peaceful rhythm; he intermingled the façades of houses and apartment buildings, signs, posters, human silhouettes—often placed on stairways—and balconies to suggest a certain depth, which in future works he was to indicate with the aid of checkerboard patterns. He varied possible combinations of shapes and objects in the excellent series on tugboats, which included such works as *The Tugboat* (Grenoble Museum) and *The Deck of the Tugboat.*[1] He continued to work on this theme until 1923, employing more static forms, as in the *Large Tugboat,* and *The Railway Station*[2] which look almost like a theatrical set.

In the article that Raynal published in "L'Esprit Nouveau" in January 1921 and that later appeared in pamphlet form, the critic underlined the importance of the solution proposed:

Fernand Léger is the first person who, through his experimental efforts with the mechanism of color, has succeeded in obtaining local color not in order to make an allusion to the dynamism of nature, but in order to transpose on to canvas the boundless activity of the world. The enthusiasm with which *The City* was greeted at the Salon des Indépendants—a work which he produced at maximum efficiency—constituted official recognition of the need for movement that is an ever-increasing factor in modern sensitivity. Instead of being merely a surface covered with a wash paint, the work of Léger is a machine—a machine which works, a play rather than a painting.

In the same issue of this journal, which was founded in October 1920 by Paul Dermée, two newcomers, Ozenfant and Jeanneret, alias Le Corbusier, launched the movement of Purism, which, by dint of its sense of clarity and precision, held a strong appeal for Léger and caused him to abandon for the moment his obsession with machinery.

The year 1920 also witnessed the forceful introduction of the human figure into his work. At first this new approach was timid, and the figures retained the appearance of machines—*Woman and Mirror* (Moderna Museet, Stockholm), *The Three Comrades* (Stedelijk Museum, Amsterdam). He also retained the factory environment, as illustrated by such paintings as *Two Men on a Scaffold* and *Man with a Pipe* (Musée d'Art Moderne de la Ville de Paris). Soon the presence of a hieratic, schematic human figure triumphed over a simple background of geometric motifs, as in the resolute statement *The Mechanic* (National Gallery, Ottawa), planned back in 1918, or in the series on women, which he continued to develop, such as *Reclining Woman.* Three works in this series were exhibited at the

1) See p. 42
2) See p. 43

26

THE MECHANIC IN THE FACTORY, 1918
Oil on canvas   25″ × 20 1/2″ (63.5 × 52 cm)
Collection: Mr. and Mrs. James W. Alsdorf, Chicago

Salon des Indépendants, in particular *Women Indoors*.[1] This heralded the majestic peak of this achievement in *Three Women* (Museum of Modern Art, New York), and lofty cadences. At the same time he was taking steps to evolve another series, of a modest format, which he called animated landscapes; in these, such as *Animated Landscape* he situated small human figures in the center of a panorama that was half rural, half urban.

During the next few years new themes emerged in Léger's art. As was the case with his previous series on women, some of these were particularly well delineated. This was true, for instance, of his still lifes such as *Still Life Candlestick*, 1922 (Musée d'Art Moderne de la Ville de Paris), *Composition and Still Life* (1923), and *Still Life with Statue* (1924). More and more he endowed his still lifes with an objective reality, a rigid and unblemished order that resembled the style of the Purists. This was also true of the landscapes, a theme that he painted less frequently. After 1924 he rarely attempted pure geometrical abstractions, as in *Mural Composition*.

All these endeavors reflect both Léger's curiosity about everything around him and his personal preoccupations. Through his involvement with "L'Esprit Nouveau" he became acquainted with Ozenfant, whom he encouraged at the start of his career and who from 1924 onward taught with him in an open workshop—where Marie Laurencin and Exter also gave instruction—prior to opening the Académie Moderne at 86 Rue Notre-Dame-des-Champs in 1929. Léger also came to know Jeanneret (Le Corbusier); they held similar opinions on the future of architecture and collaborated in the creation of the "L'Esprit Nouveau" pavilion at the Exhibition of Decorative Arts in 1925, and subsequently took several trips together. While he was working on the sets for the film "L'Inhumaine," he became associated with the architect Mallet-Stevens, who with some difficulty managed to get the abstract panel that he had ordered from Léger accepted for the entrance foyer of the pavilion of a French embassy, also at the 1925 Exhibition. In 1921, Léger established relations with members of the De Stijl group, including Mondrian and particularly Van Doesburg, whose ideas on urban planning and social issues interested him.

As for his own output, Léger remained faithful to his original aspirations and daily devoted more attention to monumental art, as was evidenced by his participation in a decorative project for an entrance hall at the 1923 Salon des Indépendants and even more by the sets and costumes for the Swedish Ballet, for which he took responsibility on two different occasions: in 1922 for "Skating Rink," and in 1923 for "The Creation of the World," based on a libretto by his friend Cendrars. For Léger this represented the long-sought opportunity to give free rein to his creative verve, his flights of poetic fancy and his artistic imagination; and he was to see at last, animated by actual movement, his fragments of reality, his cut-up planes, his geometric overlapping patterns, and the abstract motifs that he was using by 1924 in the woodcuts he did to illustrate Malraux's "Paper Moons."

Around this time he also took up his cudgel once more to defend contemporary art and justify his views on it. At the beginning of 1923, he wrote two articles for Berlin journals: a particularly important one for "Der Querschnitt" on "The Aesthetics of the Machine," which was reprinted almost immediately in New York, Paris, and Antwerp, and another on "Current Artistic Trends," published in "Das Kunstblatt." The following year he gave two lectures, one at the Sorbonne on "The Show" and the other at the

1) See p. 46

28

SOLDIER WITH A PIPE, 1916
Oil on canvas   51 1/8″ × 38 1/4″ (130 × 97 cm)
Kunstsammlung Nordrhein-Westfalen, Düsseldorf, Germany

THE CIRCUS, 1918
Oil on canvas   22 7/8″ × 37 1/4″ (58 × 94.5 cm)
Musée National d'Art Moderne
CNAC Georges Pompidou, Paris

DISCS, 1918
Oil on canvas   94 3/8″ × 70 3/4″ (240 × 180 cm)
Musée d'Art Moderne de la Ville de Paris

THE ACROBATS IN THE CIRCUS, 1918
Oil on canvas   13″ × 16 1/8″ (33 × 41 cm)
Kunstmuseum, Basel, Switzerland. Gift of Raoul La Roche

32

Collège de France on "The Aesthetics of the Machine," the texts of which were published in Vienna, Paris, and Potsdam. Léger expanded his previous ideas on the subject and distinguished two modes of artistic expression: the "art object," in the form of painting and sculpture, "which has inherent worth derived from its intensity and concentrated density, which is non-decorative, the opposite of a wall"; and "ornamental art," which he had already applied to his ballet work, "which depends on an architectural structure . . . and uses abstract and colorful flat surfaces and indicates volume through architectural and sculptural masses." He was to return frequently to this notion, which he was the first to enunciate and which he implemented from 1925 onward. Inherent in it was the notion that color could be applied to the interior or exterior of a place to create a new architectural space, that color served "a social function, a necessary function," that it should be allowed to penetrate factories, banks, and hospitals and thus "make the surfaces it touches sublime and give buildings and cities a joyous appearance." With his feeling for poetry and his confidence in a bright future, he heralded "life-giving color, polychromatic hospitals, polychromatic architecture, including all forms of everyday advertising" in the street and in the city.

Above all, he wanted to explain his position, for he was disturbed by his constant clashes with the informed public, who did not understand his work any better than the "unsophisticated, ordinary people" among whom he preferred to live. In reference to the mechanical components of which, he wrote, he was the "first to make pictorial use," they brought him, as he himself readily confessed, such violently hostile criticism in 1918–19 that he felt obliged to state that in his opinion they were "only a means and not an end," that he regarded them "simply as raw material on which to draw, just as the components of a landscape or a still life were." However, he continued to believe that machines were "certainly appropriate for anyone seeking to create a work of art with breadth and depth." As a final word, he took up this theme anew in 1924–25 in several works, such as *Mechanical Elements,*[1] *Mechanical Elements on a Red Background* (Biot Museum), and *Composition* (Solomon Guggenheim Museum, New York). Declaring war on "the prejudices which blind three-quarters of the population," on "beauty considered as something to be catalogued and categorized," Léger observed that in his day beauty might be found anywhere in the new order of "mechanical architecture," in "the polychromatic machine-objects" (automobiles, agricultural machinery, manufactured articles), in the art displayed in store windows, or in the displays at the Paris Fair. He concluded that a "picture should equal and even surpass in beauty a handsome industrial product; it should even be an organic event."

He attacked with special fervor what he considered to be the two most deadly sins committed both by artists and by the public, namely, a tendency to imitate and seek out beautiful subjects. He observed that "if a subject is beautiful, it is no longer raw material . . . therefore it cannot be used . . . it cannot even be copied." In his desire not to be bound by the canons of conventional wisdom or to be seduced by orthodoxy or sensual appeals, he went so far as to commit himself totally to the structural severity of the machine and "an authoritative geometric order" with his series of fulsome robot-men, one of which is *Women Reading*[2] and which disconcerted even his dealer, Léonce Rosenberg. If he was

1) See p. 48
2) See p. 53

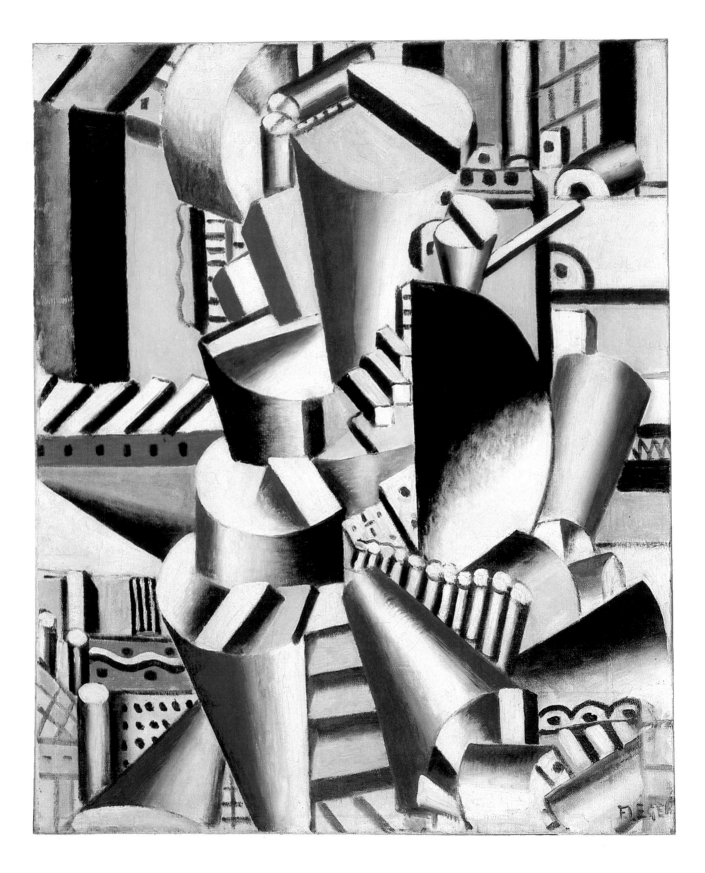

34

THE CITY, 1919
Oil on canvas
90 3/4″ × 117 1/4″ (230.5 × 297.7 cm)
Philadelphia Museum of Art. The A. E. Gallatin Collection

THE WOODEN PIPE, 1918
Oil on canvas   32″ × 26″ (81.3 × 66 cm)
Collection: William R. Acquavella, New York

35

The Scaffolding, 1919
Pen and gouache   9" × 5 7/8" (23 × 15 cm)

troubled by "the difficulty faced by the artist in choosing which raw materials to use," it would take a psychologist to analyze the impulses which drove him—as was also true of Picasso in the same period—to prefer voluptuous female forms which were frequently unappreciated by spectators.

The best insight is perhaps offered by something he wrote in 1922, which was eloquent and expressed with his usual candor, while clearly defining his goals and the problems besetting him:

My ambition is to achieve the maximum pictorial effect, using all sorts of contrasting artistic methods. So much for proper behavior, taste and *recognized* style . . . All at once I am creating something alive. For me a picture is the opposite of a wall, that is to say, it is brilliance and movement. I am happy if a picture of mine dominates a room in an apartment, if it overwhelms everything else, the people and the furniture. It must be the most important feature of the room. I detest painting. As for my subjects, I take them anywhere I find them. I like the forms invented by modern industry and I make use of them, of steel with its thousand colorful reflections, more subtle and yet more solid than so-called classical subjects. I maintain that a machine gun and the breech of a 75 mm Howitzer are more appropriate subjects for paintings than four apples on a table or a landscape of Saint-Cloud, and that does not mean indulging in Futurism . . . The Primitives have shown us that the most beautiful stories can serve as inspiration for the most beautiful pictures, but the Primitives knew how to absorb their subjects, since they *invented forms.* That is the whole point . . . Basically, it is the female nude who has turned everything upside down. It is the excess of sensuality. What can we do to resist this? I believe strongly in the lasting, durable impression which can be made on men by *the manufactured object;* if there is to be a Renaissance, therein lies its secret. The man who lives for a long time amidst serious geometric manifestations will *unconsciously*

MEN IN THE CITY, 1919
Oil on canvas   57 3/8″ × 44 5/8″ (146 × 113.5 cm)
The Peggy Guggenheim Collection, Venice. The Solomon R. Guggenheim Foundation

be won over. We should be aware of that; I am, completely. *The contemporary milieu* is, frankly, a manufactured and mechanical environment; it is slowly subjugating the breasts and the curves of women, fruits, blurred landscapes, which have been the daily bread of painters from time immemorial. Engineers and other scientists who do not understand anything about our works are, unwittingly, their defenders. It is a fine irony, but it is a fact: man as a psychological condition has less and less effect on us, but what he "manufactures" acts on us slowly but implacably. Note that it is not a question of painting the objects he offers us, but the spirit of these objects is the spirit of the times and enables us, under any and all circumstances, to benefit from their synthetic and relative qualities.

Léger was not wrong in reckoning that he could soon achieve the degree of synthesis of which he dreamed. Several exhibitions were to help him make the point as far as he was personally concerned and would revive those pictorial ambitions that had been somewhat quiescent during the period 1923–26, which might be called his architectural or Purist period, during which he devoted himself almost exclusively to depicting objects: in 1925 an exhibition at the Anderson Galleries in New York, in 1926 exhibitions at the Brooklyn Museum and at the Galerie des Quatre-Chemins in Paris, and also a retrospective at the Salon des Indépendants. In 1928 he had two showings: a very important one in Berlin at the Flechtheim Gallery and the other in Paris at the Galerie de l'Effort Moderne. In order to free himself from this many-faceted cycle in which somewhat ironically he mixed Purism, Cubism, and even—surprisingly—Super-Realism, he turned more and more to films for his inspiration, following a now familar path. Thus, he terminated the brilliant festival of still lifes conceived in accordance with a strict mechanical scheme and executed with cut-up vertical planes in a lofty, rigorous, and often very colorful style, such as *Umbrella and Bowler*.

We know that the appeal of films had manifested itself even before the war. In 1921 Léger collaborated with Cendrars in "The Wheel" and in 1923 he made a very effective contribution with his set for "L'Inhumaine." But it was in 1924 that he was able to satisfy his passion completely and put to the test his ideas on the role of movable sets, the plastic arts, and objects and ballet as spectacles, a thesis that he had expounded at length in his lectures. At that time he made use of his own resources and, with the help of Man Ray and Dudley Murphy for the photography, gave a remarkable demonstration of the possibilities offered by this technique in a short film, "Ballet Mécanique," dedicated exclusively to movement, gestures, and commonplace objects, frequently split up and seen in close-up, in an ambience appropriate to the title. Later he commented on the assignment as follows:

The entire film is constructed around the contrasts between objects, slow and rapid passages, rest and intense activity. The close-up was the only cinematographic invention I used. I also used *fragments* of objects. By isolating them, *I personalized* them. All of this work has led me to consider *the realization of objectivity* as a very effective and hitherto unrecognized virtue. Documentaries and newsreels are replete with a great many very fine "objective facts" which one only needs to gather up and interpret. We are experiencing the *advent* of the objects featured in the shops that adorn our streets.

More specifically, through his painting he was to deliver the prophetic exhortation that he promised in one of his lectures in 1924: "The future will bring about the personification of the enlarged detail, the individualization of the fragment . . . Films contribute to this respect for life. The hand is a multiple object which can be transformed. Before having seen one in the cinema, I did not really know just what a hand was! The simple object is capable of becoming something absolute, moving, tragic."

As early as 1927 the enlarged detail—flower, branch, leaf, playing cards, arm, head—appeared and established a new kind of space by using wavy lines with contrasting vertical thrusts that soon filled up the entire surface of a large, rigidly structured painting, as in *Leaves and Shells,*[1] and *Composition with Leaf* (Biot Muscum). As was his custom, these resembled a veritable profession of faith. *Composition with Hand and Hats,* for example, is related to "Ballet Mécanique," with its repetitive series, as Garaudy noted.

At this point, a fresh wind blew through his work and enlivened it, sweeping into the past the omnipresent sterility of the machine and gradually bringing about drastic changes in his art. A wave of cheerfulness washed over his paintings, rounding the contours and modulating the harmony, while chiaroscuro joyously intensified the relief, causing it to stand out clearly. His composition became lighter and more supple, abandoning its solemn heaviness; contrasting forms had a tendency to have softer outlines and almost to soar. For he had the idea, which one may well call inspired and was undoubtedly suggested by films or the stage, to implement a new concept of space: he introduced into his paintings indeterminate and boundless space. This freely enabled him to draw symbols or figures in a fantastic ballet whose appearance, even though it was based on reality, was no longer subject to earthly laws and could, if he so desired, be raised to the level of a truly poetic creation, total and absolute in its lyricism. This important decision overcame the last hurdle standing in the way of a mode of expression that owed nothing to anyone, and an individual style to which everyone could relate by the mounting success of his Academy. With his familiar irony, which should not be misinterpreted, the artist commented on the decision that led him to this period of "objects in space": "I took an object, I did away with the table, I put the object in the air, without support and without perspective." He previously explained: "I have scattered objects in space and have connected them with one another while causing them to radiate from the foreground of the painting. This is a simple game of rhythm and harmony made up of primary colors and planes, conducting lines, distances and contrasts."

He moved forward with great strides and between 1927 and 1929 easily spanned the distance between the various nudes, or the rigid and massive women against a red background, and those svelte and soaring silhouettes of *The Dance.*[2] In 1928 he produced a work which was lively and airy, albeit somewhat busy: *Still Life with Pipe on an Orange Background.* For all this he still avoided systematic and dogmatic opinions and devoted himself to experimentation or frequently did new versions of pictures with which he was satisfied. While he took pleasure in making fun of the Surrealists by bringing about "unusual encounters" between various objects such as manufactured goods—an umbrella, a straw hat, keys, as in *Still Life with Two Keys*[3]—and human figures, whose

1) See p. 55
2) See p. 58
3) See p. 56

Disc, 1918
Oil on canvas   25″ × 20 1/2″ (65 × 54 cm) Collection: Thyssen-Bornemisza, Lugano, Switzerland

presence he continued to emphasize *(The Two Dancers)*[1], he nevertheless made certain that the dancers still had one foot on the ground or at least on the receding lines which checker the painting *(Dancer in Blue)*[2] before he allowed symbols and people to frolic mysteriously in the air among fluttering ribbons *(Mona Lisa with Keys*[3]*)*.

His work was now completely liberated and continued to blossom over the years. It incorporated many details drawn with meticulous care from nature—a holly leaf, a rose, a tree trunk—and then suddenly turned to the monumental, as in *The Bather, Composition with Three Faces,* and *Marie the Acrobat.* During this time Léger established a closer relationship with the architectural milieu while on a trip to Greece with Le Corbusier in 1933 for a convention of the International Congress of Modern Architecture and attempted to persuade them to endorse his theories. It was also at this period in his life that he instinctively began to collect the studies and make the numerous preparations for the vast project that were eventually to be carried out, such as *Three Musicians,* the final version of which would be completed in 1944 (Museum of Modern Art, New York), *Parrots,* and *Adam and Eve,* the large paintings he worked on from 1935 to 1939.

Léger's intense activity henceforth earned him an international reputation. From 1932 to 1935 he was a professor at the Académie de la Grande Chaumière; at the same time, with the assistance of Nadia Khodossevitch, he was teaching in his own studio, which, because of the influx of pupils, he had to move in succession to the Rue de la Sablière, the Rue du Moulin-Vert, and the Square Henri-Delormel, where Bauquier took on the duties of treasurer. He worked in London on the sets for an H. G. Wells film and gave lectures in France and other countries, to which he frequently traveled to attend exhibitions of his work. In 1931 and 1935, for instance, he went to New York, where the Museum of Modern Art ensured the establishment of his reputation. He also visited Sweden, where he had an exhibition shortly afterward, and Zurich, where his works were on show at the Kunsthaus. During a single year, 1938, he had exhibitions in London and Paris, and in 1939 in Brussels, London, and New York.

A triumphant hymn to the commonplace

Léger returned to the United States at the beginning of 1936 and, cheered by his previous success there, by the spectacle of American life, and by the friendly reputation accorded him by some intellectuals, he did not doubt that his hour was at hand and that he would soon have more opportunity for socially relevant work. The formation of the Popular Front in France shortly thereafter raised his hopes still further.

Using the untidy outline of the aloe for contrast, he had recently allowed his landscapes and his small compositions an all-embracing lyricism that twisted and swelled: trees, flowers, butterflies, and clouds gave his pictures a flamboyant and abstract appearance which, when complemented by the richness of his colors, made them unexpectedly

1) See p. 59
2) See p. 54
3) See p. 61

THE DECK OF THE TUGBOAT, 1920
Oil on canvas   38″ × 51 1/8″ (96.5 × 130 cm)
Musée National d'Art Moderne
CNAC Georges Pompidou, Paris

43

BREAKFAST, 1922
Oil on canvas   25 1/2″ × 36 1/4″ (65 × 92 cm)
Collection: Stephen Hahn, New York

RECLINING WOMAN, 1921
Oil on canvas   19 3/4″ × 25 5/8
(50 × 65 cm)
Collection: Mr. and Mrs. Klaus Perls, New York

WOMEN INDOORS, 1921
Oil on canvas   25 3/8″ × 36 1/4″ (64.5 × 92 cm)
Musée National d'Art Moderne
CNAC Georges Pompidou, Paris

Mother and Child, 1922
Pencil drawing   9 1/2″ × 12 1/4″ (24 × 31 cm)
Louise Leiris Gallery, Paris

46

appealing. In 1935 he paid tribute to sport through an imposing mural that he produced for the World Exhibition in Brussels, for a gymnasium to be built under the direction of Charlotte Perriand. He constructed a joyous ballet of objects in which, before outstretched arms, there paraded in a sinuous procession a wide variety of gymnastic equipment, such as dumbbells, a ball, bars, a ladder, rope and so on. Jean Cassou asked him the reason for this vast work, and he justified himself in this way: "Rather than return to a subject, it is a good idea to appeal to an *object*. Painting which depends on an object takes on social significance. It becomes accessible to everyone and can be used in schools, stadiums, and public monuments." At its birth, he was a patron of the Salon de l'Art Mural founded by Saint Maur and participated in its successive showings in 1935, 1936, and 1938.

Unfortunately, it was not long before hope turned to disappointment. The Paris World Exhibition of 1937 ignored his various projects and by way of compensation commissioned him to produce only one—albeit immense—mural for the Palais de la Découverte. This was *The Transportation of Power,* in which he combined pylons and transformers with a tumultuous nature, sublimating them under a sovereign rainbow. In spite of the insistence with which he tried to advance the artistic education of the masses, the new regime did not seem eager to implement his ideas, and the working classes

MECHANICAL
ELEMENTS, 1924
Oil on canvas
57 1/2″ × 38 1/4″
(146 × 97 cm)
Musée National
d'Art Moderne
CNAC
Georges Pompidou,
Paris

remained indifferent to his appeals and his on-the-spot presentations. While futile and interminable debates were raging on "The Argument about Realism," he intervened to defend modern art by reminding the public: "We have liberated color and geometric forms. They have conquered the world. This New Realism has been in command for the last fifty years, in easel painting as well as in decorative art, both indoor and outdoor." And he announced: "We are faced with the possibility of creating and executing a new type of collective mural art."

He derived singular satisfaction from his work on some projects he had often expressed the desire to do, such as creating the décor for two popular festivals in the Vélodrome d'Hiver—one organized in 1937 by the trade unions, the other, more imaginative, in 1939 for the production of a play by J. R. Block, "Birth of a City."

Even if account is taken of the other assignments which he was given—for the Paris Opera—the sets for a ballet by Serge Lifar, "David Triumphant," in 1937, and the decoration of the New York apartment of Nelson A. Rockefeller, Jr., in 1938, his output over this four-year period was limited. Such a sparse inventory must have appeared preposterously small to the man who proclaimed the triumph of "Color in the World" in Antwerp in 1937 and "Color in Architecture" in the course of eight lectures which he delivered at Yale University in 1938. In Antwerp he gave public expression to his feeling of regret in a noble and prophetic statement: "The honor of modern society depends on its being strong and generous enough to afford the luxury of permitting some individuals whose work will be recognized and admired at a later date to operate freely."

It is understandable that he found it difficult to disregard this partial failure in the field of monumental art, although he was given several exhibitions, and difficult to complete two major paintings on which he had been working since 1935 (*Adam and Eve*[1] and *Composition with Two Parrots*[2]). In both of these, he wanted to achieve a synthesis of all his aspirations, and *Composition with Two Parrots* was a canvas of vaster dimensions than any he had worked on prior to that time. In both instances, and in particularly spectacular fashion in the case of the larger picture, he succeeded in presenting an idyllic vision, embellished by an exotic touch, of his traditional mechanic, who still had a somewhat severe appearance but one relieved now by his having acquired the bearing of a sportsman, accompanied by a spritely comrade or a dancer and acrobats. All of them have their feet set firmly on the ground amidst flowers, ropes, posts, and fences on which clothes are hung—but all of them are proud and distant, their heads held high in the air, amid fluffy clouds jostling against one another. This was an admirable and striking introduction to Léger's ambition to restore, in uncertain and perilous times, a sense of the dignity of human beings through the enchantment of a delicately shaded rainbow of colors.

Taken unawares first by war, then by defeat, Léger went from city to city attempting to flee from the Nazis whom he had fought for so long, and in October 1940 he managed to board a ship in Marseilles bound for New York, where his many friends helped him to find a place to live and work. Although he obtained a teaching chair at Yale and, soon afterwards, one at Mills College in California, he nevertheless led the somewhat lonely existence that was the fate of so many of his fellow refugees, despite the fact that among the displaced artists there were quite a few who had been his friends, such as Chagall,

1) See p. 70
2) See p. 71

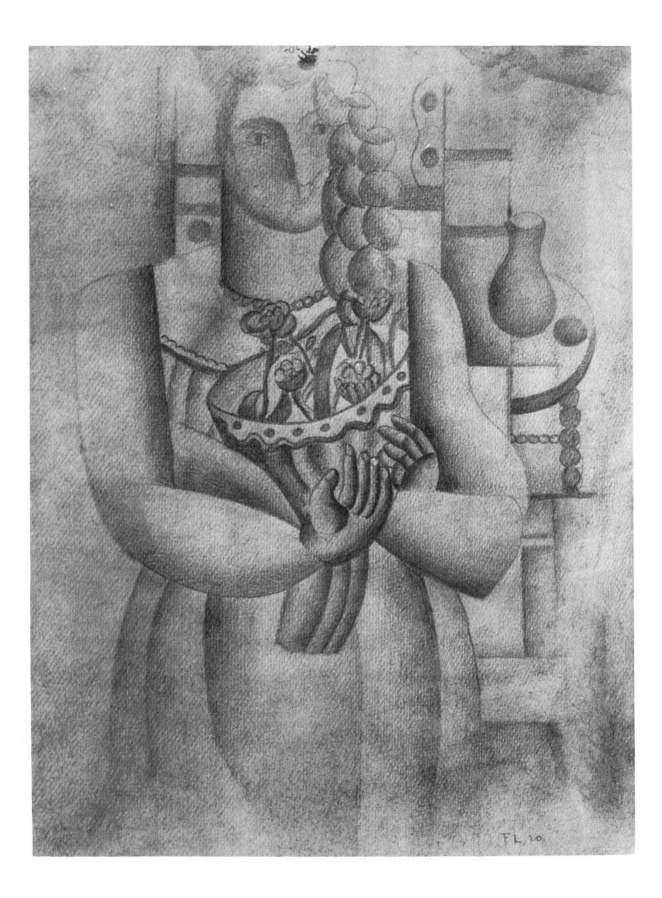

50

The Three Musicians, 1920
Drawing

Woman with Flowers, 1920
Pencil drawing   15" × 11 3/8" (38 × 29 cm)
Louise Leiris Gallery, Paris

Woman Holding Flowers, 1924
Black ink on paper   10 1/2″ × 5″ (26.7 × 12.7 cm)
Collection: Mr. and Mrs. Gordon Bunshaft, New York

Ozenfant, Mondrian, and Zadkine. He confirmed this in the recollections that he shared with the author later. He found it hard to endure exile, not to receive news, to have to change his daily pattern of existence, especially his eating habits—he made an amusing reference to the latter in the film that Thomas Bouchard made about him.

At the first threat of war he experienced a feeling of melancholy, of mental anguish even. Without his being aware of it, this colored some of his compositions, especially the still lifes, which were filled with angular, roughly broken lines, knotty, twisted, gaping, sawtoothed forms, and with partly symbolic elements, such as a root, a tree trunk, a wheel, a broken ladder, a scythe, or a chain. On the whole, he borrowed very little directly from the American landscape, except the opulence of nature and piles of rubbish.

Rather, he was inspired by the familiar universe of his drawings and paintings which, fortunately, he had been able to take with him to America, probably hoping that, by digging into his exile's luggage, he would be able to overcome a futile nostalgia. By working diligently, in the five years of his stay he was able to produce close to 120 pictures, and during this time galleries and museums vied with one another to acquire his work and to exhibit it, particularly in New York but also in Chicago, Oakland, Montreal, Cincinnati, and Cambridge. As he observed in 1942, in what was perhaps a slightly biased view: "My work continues to develop and is in no way dependent on where I am situated geographically. What I am painting here could equally well have been

WOMEN READING, 1924
Oil on canvas   45″ × 57 1/2″ (114 × 146 cm)
Musée National d'Art Moderne
CNAC Georges Pompidou, Paris

DANCER IN BLUE, 1930
Oil on canvas   78 3/4″ × 55 1/8″ (200 × 140 cm)
Musée National d'Art Moderne, CNAC Georges Pompidou, Paris

54

LEAVES AND SHELLS, 1927
Oil on canvas   51″ × 38 1/4″ (129.5 × 98.5 cm) The Tate Gallery, London

STILL LIFE WITH TWO KEYS, 1930
Oil on canvas   57 1/2″ × 38 1/4″ (146 × 97 cm)
Musée National d'Art Moderne, CNAC Georges Pompidou, Paris

painted in Paris or London. The milieu does not affect me at all. A work of art is the result of an inner motivation and owes nothing to the picturesqueness of its surroundings. Perhaps the tempo of New York or the climate enables me to work *faster*. That is all."

He was still working under the impetus that had begun to affect him before the war. The same passion for monumental art absorbed him, was the focal point of his thoughts, and would continue to occupy his mind until the end of his life.

He had barely landed when, in December 1940, the Museum of Modern Art offered to exhibit his impressive *Composition with Two Parrots;* this appeared to him to be a good omen, as was the review published shortly thereafter in "Muralist." At Mills College, in the summer of 1941, he was the beneficiary of a "huge exhibition" in which he showed several of his important recent pictures, according to the account given by Darius Milhaud, who soon afterward proposed that he do the sets for the opera "Bolivar," which he was just finishing. Other ideas were also

Composition, 1926
Ink drawing   10 3/4" × 8 1/4" (27 × 21 cm)
Louise Leiris Gallery, Paris

taking root in the mind of Léger, who sketched some proposed designs for the décor of Radio City and Rockefeller Center and was already looking forward to projects for stained-glass windows and, with Mary Callery, models of polychrome sculpture.

Without waiting for these projects to materialize—which indeed they did not—he immediately set to work on a new pictorial theme that was consistent with his previous experiments. The theme, men in space, took its inspiration from a scene witnessed on the wharfs of Marseilles, where dock workers were pushing each other into the water. From his observations of this cluster of disjointed, tangled bodies, seized in full flight, he drew numerous variations, setting off contours, relief, contrasts, and colors on canvases of imposing size. In picture after picture the same motif recurred, still treated in orderly and compact fashion, as in *Divers on a Yellow Background,*[1] painted in 1941. It reappeared during the years that followed, in reverse composition in *Acrobats in Gray,* and in *The Dance,* which exploded in a pyrotechnic display. The silhouettes became more supple and lively, bouncing like balls, bounding up like living signals *(Large Black Divers* and *Polychrome Divers).* If, in this

1) See p. 72

THE DANCE, 1930
Oil on canvas   51 1/8″ × 35 1/2″ (130 × 90 cm) Musée de Grenoble, France

THE TWO DANCERS, 1928
Oil on canvas   36 1/4″ × 28 3/4″ (92 × 73 cm) Collection: Dr. Peter Nathan, Zurich

59

Fragment of Face, 1933
Pen drawing   12 3/8″ × 9 5/8″ (31.5 × 24.5 cm) Louise Leiris Gallery, Paris

60

MONA LISA WITH KEYS, 1930
Oil on canvas 35 3/4″ × 27 3/8″ (91 × 72 cm) Musée National Fernand Léger, Biot, France

Acrobatic Dancers, 1930
Ink drawing   12 3/8″ × 14 1/2″ (30.5 × 37 cm)
Louise Leiris Gallery, Paris

Old Gloves, 1930
Drawing with india ink   9 5/8″ × 12 3/4″ (24.8 × 32.5 cm)
Louise Leiris Gallery, Paris

62

instance, Léger confessed that he owed something to American dynamism or to the "floodlights of Broadway sweeping the street," which taught him to stripe his pictures with layers of color that bore no relation to form—a happy innovation of which he would make repeated and very skillful use—that did not prevent him from continuing to pursue his permanent objective. He referred to it in 1942: "My final goal is to obtain a maximum amount of power and even of violence on a wall . . . I am unable to achieve this power except by the ruthless application of the most extreme contrasts, such as flat surfaces in pure colors, molded components in gray tones, and objects treated realistically."

Without really believing in it this time, he dreamed of an immense work, one which he feared would be almost impossible to paint, and one which would be the culmination of his overly ambitious cycle of men in space and which he would transform later into *The Builders*. He optimistically preferred a return to the commonplace, a need he felt deeply and unremittingly. Sometimes he delved into his memories and reclaimed some of the tentative experiments that for many years had been based on two themes—the circus and the dance band—which were inspired by reality, often combined, and at all events closely related. Once more he took them up, on a larger scale, but for the moment separating them and treating them with an amused breeziness, allowing himself the pleasure of creating several

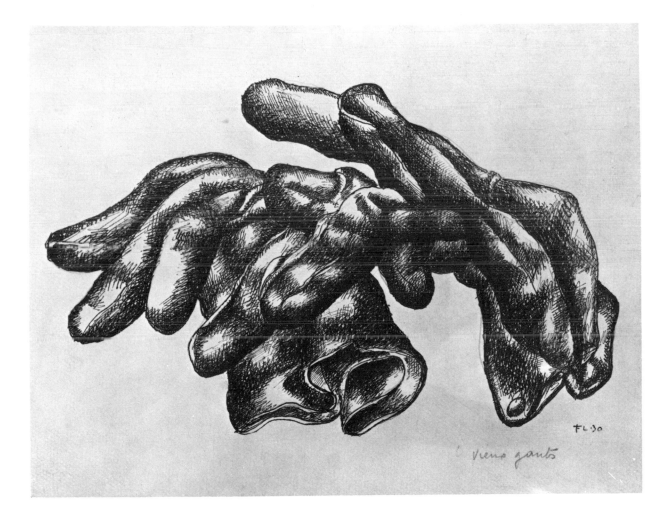

63

CONTRASTED OBJECTS, 1930
Oil on canvas   43 1/4″ × 74 3/4″ (110 × 190 cm)
Musée National d'Art Moderne
CNAC Georges Pompidou, Paris

64

versions, as in *Acrobats, Trapeze Artists,* and *Musicians.* Sometimes he observed people and their conduct directly and depicted them with unobtrusive humor and a care for detail, as in his appealing series of cyclists. Although he had previously dealt with his subject, he now diversified it and showed visible satisfaction in the accomplishment, as in *The Women Cyclists,*[1] *Big Julie,*[2] *Six People on a Red Background,* and *The Fine Team.* This led him to start to rough out his study on *Leisure.*[3] In this series there became visible in his work, distinguished by superb flat tints of eye-dazzling color, a typical and almost idyllic world, in which people, well drawn and of robust frame, but anonymous and ordinary, confidently took their place in the serenity of a peace to come. This was indeed a world that the artist had looked forward to for a long time.

Preceded by the aura of an exhibition held in January 1945 by Louis Carré (who arranged a show for him almost every year henceforth, with a particular celebration in New York in 1951, for his seventieth birthday), Léger, back in Paris in December 1945, shared the euphoria of the Liberation and the hopes that it raised. When the author saw him at that time, Léger was buoyantly happy and completely confident that his hour was at hand and that he would at long last have the opportunity to take his revenge, without the least bitterness, on a destiny that up until then had ignored his monumental projects. Accessible to everyone, as was his wont, he gave numerous interviews and even, at the request of "Travail et Culture," agreed to give a lecture at the Sorbonne on "Art and the People," sponsored by Léon Moussinac.

No other artists of his generation or of the younger generation, who tended to isolate themselves, were as open or receptive to the many offers they received. Léger was careful not to overlook or refuse anyone and generously cooperated with everyone who asked. His activity was prodigious, as if he were trying to make up for lost time and had a premonition that he had only a few years left to live. He took obvious pleasure in satisfying all the people from all over the world who invited him to participate in various ventures such as the Salon de l'Art Mural, the Salon d'Art

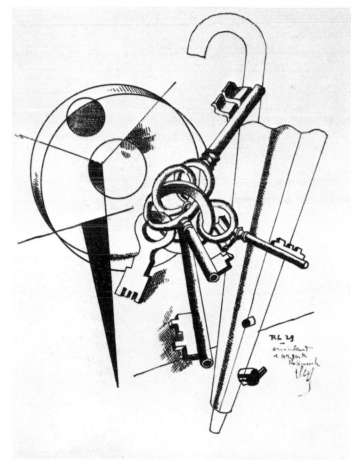

Composition with Keys, 1929
Pen   12 1/4″ × 9″ (31 × 23.5 cm)

1) See p. 69
2) See p. 77
3) See p. 78

Sacré, the Maison de la Pensée Française, and the Salon de Mai, to which he sent pictures regularly, the galleries and museums in different countries which wished to show his work, the events and biennial exhibitions held throughout the world to pay homage to Cubism and to the masters of contemporary art. Great cities vied with one another for the honor of devoting retrospectives to his work, such as Stockholm in 1948, Paris in 1949, London in 1951, Amsterdam and Berne in 1952, Chicago and New York in 1953, and Lyons and Rio de Janeiro in 1955. With an equal show of pleasure he plunged anew into theatrical decoration and successfully executed a number of stage sets: in 1948 for the ballet "Le Pas d'Acier" at the Théâtre des Champs-Elysées; in 1949 for "Bolivar" at the Paris Opera, a project that had been planned for a long time; and in 1952 for a ballet by his neighbor, Janine Charrat, at Amboise. Shortly before, in 1950, he did illustrations for Rimbaud's "Illuminations," and above all "The Circus," published by Tériade, in which he worked wonders with the text and produced the lithographs with a corresponding zest. In 1953 he also did the illustrations for the poem "Liberty" by Paul Eluard.

This fiendishly energetic man managed to be everywhere at once. Every Friday he corrected the work done by the pupils at his Academy, which had reopened in Montrouge before his return to France, and soon had to move to the Boulevard de Clichy because of the influx of students (whom he frequently put to work on his current projects, such as the temporary décor they did in 1948 at the Porte de Versailles for the International Congress of Women). In 1949 he went to Biot with his former pupil Roland Brice to design their first ceramics together. A year later, they set up a small factory-workshop there. In 1952 he married Nadia Khodossevich, who had helped him for many years, and they settled in Gif-sur-Yvette, at Gros Tilleul. But at the same time he also traveled: in 1948 he went to Poland for the Peace Congress in Wrocław and to Belgium, where he was persuaded to attend a debate on "The Art of Today" with Jean Bazaine and the author before an audience of residents of Brussels and Antwerp. In 1951 he went to Milan for the Triennale, in 1952 to Berne for a lecture and to Venice for the Biennale, and in 1955 to Prague for the Congress of Sokols.

Such a life, so hectic and busy, somehow satisfied the particular needs of his nature and, even more important, enabled him to meet many of the demands that he deemed essential. On his return, he quickly realized that, after five years of absence and the inevitable oblivion that this produced, and in spite of the invaluable support of Carré and soon thereafter of Maeght, he would have to struggle to regain his supremacy and reaffirm his ever solitary position. In order to do this, he would have to wage war against the two opposition movements that at that time were strenuously vying for preeminence: Abstractionism and Social Realism. In his lectures—in 1948 at the Sorbonne on "The Problem of Realism in Modern Painting" and in 1952 at the Maison de la Pensée Française, he remained faithful to his original principles and was not afraid to incur the wrath of the Communist party, of which he had become a member and which at that moment was excommunicating any artists or critics who supported Abstractionism. To this end he declared, with admirable clairvoyance, in a survey made for "Les Amis de l'Art" in 1947: "Personally, I see an important development in this abstract art in that it can be adapted to architecture and used on walls. If abstract art hopes to have any future, it should pay attention to this aspect of its use."

In his pictorial work, too, he resisted the temptation to succumb to the pressure of topical subjects, such as Nazi atrocities, the Resistance effort, and labor unrest, to which so many, including some of the most famous artists, were devoting their work. He constantly used as motifs subjects drawn from everyday life which he ennobled through the magic of his distinctive touch. In 1948–49 he returned to the familiar theme of cyclists, rendering the pictures still more forceful by the vigor of his flat tints and their clear-cut chromatic gradation, brilliantly contrasting with the deep ultramarine background. He christened the work *Leisure, Homage to David,* in order to underline the spirit of continuity to which he was faithful and his loyalty to the great traditions of the past. Soon thereafter he produced a fragmentary variation, *The Two Cyclists,* in which the color was completely liberated. If, in order to relax, he sometimes returned to the spontaneous lyricism of his traditional still lifes, such as compositions featuring a branch or a tree or a woman with a bird, he also plunged into surprising and unexpected innovations. Among these, beginning in 1947, was a series of fragmentary faces, emerging between spread fingers, which he called

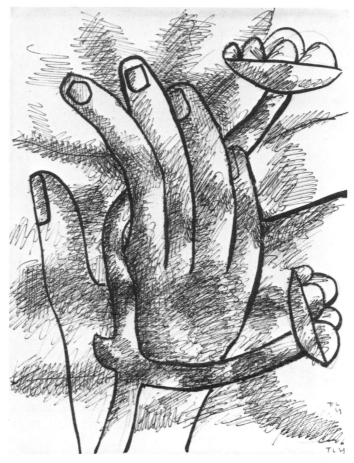

Hands and Flowers, 1931
Ink   15 3/8″ × 12 1/4″ (39 × 31 cm)

portraits (*Portrait of Eluard, Portrait of Nadia*), outlined by thick black borders crossed by lively colored stripes. Later, innovations appeared in his landscapes, which alternated between an appealing bareness and a multitude of pylons and telephone wires with birds perched on them. Moved by the omnipresent desire always to stay as close as possible to reality, he took a major step forward in 1950 in his huge work *The Builders,* which seemed, at least superficially, to be just what was expected of him, since it was offered to the Renault workers, who were slightly disappointed. (A smaller version was subsequently given to the Pushkin Museum in Moscow.) Together with the meticulous drawings, the preliminary sketches,[1] and the successive drafts, which followed one another at such a speed that Bauquier later made a film from them, he combined, as was customary with him, the recent visual recollection of a building yard perceived on a road in the Chevreuse valley as well as the theme that he had used ever since 1920 of workers on scaffolding or in a factory and also his cycle of men in space, which was so dear to him. His goal, in his own words, was not "to make a single artistic concession" or to portray the subjects of "incidents which speedily become out of date," even if he gave greater individuality to

1) See p. 80

his faces and postures, but, as he stated precisely and with dignity: "I wished to illustrate... the contrast between man and his inventions, between the worker and all the metallic architecture, the concrete, the scrap iron, the bolts and the rivets. I have situated the clouds where they belong technically, but I have also made them serve as a contrast to the beams. No concession to sentiment..." It is true that this metal scaffolding plays a major role superbly: While it reaches out in every direction, it still occupies the stage front and center. Its structural components, painted in intense colors or audaciously left pure white, stand out against the blue of the background and fill the whole space. And finally, his skillful arrangements of various interlacing patterns cannot fail to remind the viewer how much they owe to the mechanical structures of an earlier period.

During the next few years, Léger once more returned to the people with whom he was familiar as subjects for his paintings, to a peaceful and happily relaxed world such as that evoked in *Leisure*. He produced two enormous paintings that were alike in their conception and had similar variants but came to a different conclusion: in 1953 *The Picnic*[1] (Maeght Foundation), inspired by a 1943 drawing, in the different versions of which he recalled the bold American scape, and in 1954 *The Camper* (Biot Museum), whose orderly composition was reinforced by the introduction of pylons and balusters. By their vastness, the majesty of their composition and the richness of their colors, these works bear witness to Léger's formidable vitality: the first was exhibited both at the Maison de la Pensée Française and at a show arranged in Léger's honor at the Salon de Mai, while the second received first prize at the São Paulo Biennial in 1955. At the same time, after a variety of preliminary versions, Léger finished a work of exceptional size, *The Great Parade*.[2]

It can truthfully be said to be the masterpiece of his life, since he had nursed the idea since 1936, or even longer, and frequently revived it, as in his recent lithographs of the circus. Eventually he made it the marvellous culmination of his indefatigable experiments with space. His old dream, the one he thought would be impossible to realize, came true, as, alas, did the prophecy he made when he wrote in 1942: "My goal... would be to combine in an immense picture the two modes of artistic expression... If I can accomplish that, then I could die quietly. I would be content." The result, which was almost more than he had hoped for, was there, disconcerting in its simplicity, since Léger managed to fill his large painting with a kind of graphic effect that in a few places and with extreme skill was strongly underlined and sharpened by spots of color that point to the placement of forms or act as a contrast to the white and off-white backgrounds. The whole chromatic ambience, which is of unequaled richness and vigor, is achieved by bands, rings, and circles of pure color that crisscross the canvas and, insofar as is possible, transform and reconstitute space like spotlights, highlighting different scenes and gesturing people. None of this explains why Léger, who always evinced a passionate interest in the circus, displayed, like Picasso, such an utter fascination with clowns toward the end of his life. Should one see in this the symbolic image of a kind of spectacular auto-da-fé, or the desire to hide the artist's bitterness and disillusionment behind a comic mask, or even possibly a final peal of vengeful laughter at the foibles of society?

If we limit ourselves to a discussion of Léger's painting technique, which preoccupied him constantly, it is apparent that another factor was partly responsible for the success that

1) See also p. 79
2) See p. 88

THE WOMEN CYCLISTS, 1944
Oil on canvas   44 1/8″ × 50 1/4″ (112 × 128.5 cm)
Collection: Nathan Cummings, New York

ADAM AND EVE, 1935–39
Oil on canvas   89 3/4″ × 127 5/8″ (228 × 324.5 cm)
Kunstsammlung Nordrhein-Westfalen, Düsseldorf, Germany

DIVERS ON A YELLOW BACKGROUND, 1941
Oil on canvas   75 3/4″ × 87 1/2″ (192.5 × 222.5 cm)
The Art Institute of Chicago. Gift of Mr. and Mrs. Maurice E. Culberg

Acrobats and Parrots. c. 1939
Drawing   26 3/4″ × 18 7/8″ (68 × 48 cm)
Charles Kriwin Gallery, Brussels

Woman Reading, 1931
Pencil drawing   20 5/8″ × 21″ (52.5 × 61 cm)
Louise Leiris Gallery, Paris

74

he achieved, a decisive occurrence that brought him the most profound satisfaction and was the glorious apotheosis of all his aspirations and efforts. This was the sudden influx of commissions for murals during the last years of his life.

It all began, somewhat indirectly, when in 1946 R. P. Couturier unexpectedly asked him to decorate the façade of the church of Notre-Dame du Plateau d'Assy, for which he had already obtained the cooperation of painters such as Bonnard, Matisse, and Rouault. In spite of the heavy columns that the architect Novarina had included, Léger succeeded in marking the immense mosaic with his habitual overlapping patterns of blues, reds, and yellows. This superb, effective mural was dominated by a head of the Virgin, through which he recalled the admiration he felt when he visited the Byzantine churches of Ravenna with Léonce Rosenberg in 1924. On the occasion of the dedication of the church in 1950, public reaction to his work was on the whole much more favorable than it was to that of Germaine Richier. Other religious commissions followed: They included seventeen windows in "dalle-de-verre,"[1] a tapestry for the church of Audincourt in the Doubs, which he finished in 1951, and some stained-glass windows that were also made by Barillet and finished in 1954 for the church of Courfaivre in Switzerland. To his virulent critics in the Communist party who fulminated against him, he replied with courage and great dignity: "Glorifying sacred objects, nails, ciboria, or crowns of thorns, depicting the drama of Christ, is not for me an equivocation... My purpose has been to achieve an evolutionary rhythm of forms and colors which would be for everyone, believers and nonbelievers alike, something useful that could be accepted by one group as well as the other, inasmuch as joy and light can in truth penetrate the heart of each individual."

While some of the many projects he conceived at the time were never realized, such as the plan for the Basilica of Peace in Sainte-Baume, first contemplated in 1946, or the plan requested by Niemeyer in 1954 for the auditorium of the São Paulo opera house, others, happily, did take concrete form and demonstrated beyond any doubt the enormous spirituality that shone forth from Léger's art, which was at the time verging on the abstract. Cases in point are the mosaics done in 1950 for the crypt of the American Memorial in Bastogne, Belgium, and, later, a huge exterior mosaic and interior polychrome designs for the Memorial Hospital of Saint-Lô, which were not finished until after his death. Finally, the government decided to give him some assignments. In 1951 he was commissioned to paint, for the French pavilion at the Milan Triennale, a gigantic mural with dynamic interlacements painted by his pupils, and in 1955 he was asked to produce a sculpture, a ceramic, and a mosaic for the use of the Gaz de France coking plant at Alfortville. He also received commissions from abroad. In 1952 he decorated the walls of the great assembly hall of the United Nations building in New York, in consultation with the architect Harrisson, with two large panels executed by Gregory in accordance with his designs; at almost the same time an Italian company commissioned a mural for the steamship "Vulcania," and in 1953 the architect Carlos Raul Villanueva asked for his assistance in decorating the new buildings of the Central University in Caracas. In this case, too, he resolved the difficult problems posed by the assignment admirably, albeit without actually going to Venezuela. First, on the esplanade of the Rectorate, in a typically tropical ambience, he had to create a mosaic on both sides of a wall several yards high that wound around the sculpture of his old friend Laurens. He thereupon fashioned a long

1) "dalle-de-verre": slab glass cast in concrete or epoxy, a technique first used and perfected by the French in the 1930s.

stretch of green and orange foliage against a white background and sent the mosaic to Venezuela ready pasted on paper. Then, not far from the Aula Magna, in which his friend Calder reigned supreme, he undertook the task of decorating the entrance hall, as high as a cathedral, of the central library, a building of seven or eight stories, with a stained-glass window. The aura of sumptuousness produced by the red tones of the blazing "dalle-de-verre," which was also made in advance, filled the immense space so successfully that a local collector, Innocente Palacios, in a burst of enthusiasm, immediately commissioned Léger to create a stained-glass window several yards high for his home, and a monumental ceramic for his swimming pool.

We should not forget that, in addition to all these successful projects that followed one another with such apparent ease on his part, since he was able to have the work performed by various specialized studios according to the numerous designs and models created by him, he also produced some sculptures in bronze and some imposing polychrome ceramics. As has been stated previously, for several years Léger undertook the chore of using ceramics for monuments. As early as 1950 he had overcome the difficulties presented by the material with which he was working, as is shown by his first large ceramic sculpture, *The Walking Flower* (Musée National d'Art Moderne, Paris). With the aid of Roland Brice he perfected a very simple procedure in which the alternating play of protuberances and grooves was underlined by black rings that enhanced the prominence of the figures or abstract forms that he had carefully created and enabled him, as he confided to Verdet, "to house sun in my ceramic works and simultaneously to give a light, airy quality to the relief." A huge panel that is embedded in the walls of La Colombe d'Or at Vence, in the South of France, and some impressive polychrome sculptures shown at two successive exhibitions, one at the Leiris Gallery in 1951 and the other at the Carré Gallery in 1953, demonstrate very well the goal he was seeking, ever faithful to his own creed, which he defined in his foreword: "Architectural collaboration. . . mural art. . . with all the possibilities it has to offer: utilization indoors and outdoors."

Far from being halted by Léger's death, which came suddenly on August 17, 1955, his innovative efforts were continued, thanks to the stubborn insistence of Nadia Léger, supported by Georges Bauquier, and they ran their term to a grandiose conclusion. The outcome, as he would have wished, was the creation of monumental art of enormous expressive power, worthy, as Malraux observed, of withstanding comparison with any work done by the Mexican muralists, whom Léger had consistently admired and sought to emulate. At the top of the building erected in Biot in 1960 by André Svetchine, to serve as a museum and to house the works donated in 1967, is a ceramic of some 3,600 square feet, executed from a model originally intended for the Olympic Stadium in Hanover; it occupies the 150-foot length of the façade which was specifically designed to accommodate it. Its dynamic and brilliant majesty immediately attracts the visitor's gaze. A little farther along, one's attention is drawn to the gigantic polychrome sculpture *Flower-Sun,* happily symbolizing a hearty welcome.

Inside, apart from the pictures and the collection of drawings, a stained-glass window about thirty feet high, several tapestries, and some ceramics retrace the inevitable itinerary that Léger's work could normally be expected to follow, even after his death, and bear eloquent testimony to the soundness of his views and his desire, from the very beginning of his career, to dedicate himself wholeheartedly to monumental art, which was so sorely needed in France and which Léger was the only person to promote.

BIG JULIE, 1945
Oil on canvas   44″ × 50 1/8″ (111.8 × 127.3 cm)
The Museum of Modern Art, New York
Acquired through the Lillie P. Bliss Bequest

LEISURE, 1948–49
Oil on canvas   61″ × 72 3/4″ (155 × 185 cm)
Musée National d'Art Moderne
CNAC Georges Pompidou, Paris

STUDY FOR THE PICNIC, 1953
Oil on canvas   44 15/16″ × 57 1/2″ (114 × 146 cm)
Collection Stephen Hahn, New York

BUILDERS WITH ROPE, 1950
Oil on canvas 63 1/2″ × 44 7/8″ (161.2 × 114 cm) Collection Evelyn Sharp, New York

80

How are we accurately to sum up and assess the true value of Léger's contribution to art? He worked for over fifty years, in an exceptional manner, with a concern for continuity and unity without equal in the realm of contemporary art, with a perseverance and feeling for craftsmanship. Indeed, Léger was fond of saying that he belonged to an artisanal tradition. But let us beware of describing him merely as a popular image-maker, however much of a genius he may have been, for by using this much abused term, one risks creating an impression that ill serves him. Even though false inferences might be drawn from the facility that was a hallmark of his work—its simplicity, its sincerity, the roughness that he deliberately made a feature of his art and of his life—beneath this superficial ease there lay hidden, as we have said, a furious amount of work, a long period of preparation and reflection and a skill of execution. Is this not invariably the case with the greatest creative artists, who succeed in giving the public the impression that they are performing their roles as "tightrope walkers," to use a favorite expression of Matisse, as if it were the easiest thing in the world, whereas they have been practicing for years!

As far as Léger himself was concerned, his only ambition was to be a good technician, to work exclusively and uncompromisingly on his paintings with a single-minded dedication that was sometimes trying even for his admirers, but on which he justifiably prided himself. Almost at the end of his life, he confided to Verdet, "I am constantly striving to remain faithful to myself by refusing ever to deviate from the path which I have taken and which is quite contrary to the ways of seduction. In fact, I believe I have departed from that path very little."

The three basic objectives that he set for himself and that dominated his aesthetic philosophy—color, space, and design—are truly inseparable and must be considered as a whole. Though they appear to be spontaneous and elementary, an integral part of his personality and temperament, we know beyond doubt that he never ceased to analyze them in order to deepen their meaning, enrich them, and change them for the better.

Thus, his powerful and unusual feeling for color became apparent early on, although completely inconsistent with the standards of the period and with everything that surrounded him. After 1913, Léger did not hesitate to use pure tones, painting startling contrasts and innovating in masterly fashion by alternating bright stripes on a white background. This, in my opinion, is one of his most extraordinarily felicitous devices, for it introduced spatial dynamics and a freedom of composition that budding Abstractionism was to ignore but which, fortunately, was later picked up by Kinetic Art. After the war Léger emphasized his chromatic plainchant still more, soon arranging wide, generous stretches of flat tints, organized more or less like meticulous works of a great clock. This met the needs of the moment and immediately gave rise at every level, as he had for so long predicted it would, to an unquenchable and almost physiological thirst for color that still exists today, since it satisfies the most profound needs of man's nature. Always using the same basic range, he nevertheless managed to diversify it gradually as he went along, to renew it by skillfully intensifying in turn the blacks, the grays, and the whites, and finally to endow it with an incomparable and splendid density, the power to produce a radiance, a fullness, a living joyousness, qualities that were features of his personality, especially during the last ten or fifteen years of his life.

Léger's virtues as a colorist, the subtle harmonies he created in spite of the contrasting tones raised to the nth degree of saturation, should not cause one to overlook the equally deft and incomparable manner with which he created space. Motivated by an instinctive need to move within the limits of reality and never to sever his links with it, he nonetheless continually strove to make the viewer aware of the third dimension. Without resorting to outdated traditional techniques, he tried therefore to suggest it, even in his abstract works, by one means or another, relying in turn on the color or the composition to emphasize the difference in planes. Thanks to his unique skill, he succeeded in accomplishing the impossible and winning the beholder over. He first planted objects, and then persons, on the ground and sent them fluttering about with remarkable ease in a spatial environment that the eye can see distinctly and which is evoked by a few artifices, such as intersecting or sliding planes and interlaced ropes, so ingeniously placed that the eye perceives them without really registering what it sees. The new space comes into view as if by magic, attracts the attention, becomes apparent, an invisible aerial envelope without limits. And finally he plays on it, as we have already pointed out, like a virtuoso. This constant preoccupation with space, a concept that he greatly respected and one which he developed in admirable fashion, was converted into a major component of his work and an important element in the field of modern art.

Faithful to the lesson learned from Cézanne, Léger was scrupulously conscientious in designing and arranging his volumes, but, influenced by the dynamism of the period and by his admiration for the development of machinery, he immediately transformed his composition into a complex set of gears in motion. Unlike so many other artists and writers of the day who were satisfied to pay lip service to the idea of movement, to extol or to ridicule the machine, he sought to understand it. He identified himself with it, penetrated it and settled down inside it, as it were. He went so far as to shape the world of living creatures in its image, even though it might be a monstrous one. He was probably ahead of his time in celebrating the hold exerted over cities and men by an industrial civilization whose inevitable constraints we are discovering only now. Nevertheless, he quickly relinquished such futile sponsorship of the purely mechanical and restored to his automatons their human aspect, without ceasing to place their hieratic silhouettes and their varied surroundings in a skillfully constructed clockworklike system in which nothing was left to chance and movement was naturally and coherently orchestrated. His composition, particularly when he was able to spread it across large surfaces, from that moment on actually breathed, and its irresistible fervor was marked by a pulsating majesty.

Thus everything finally came together—the intensity of color and contrasts, the perception of space, a rhythmic structure—to enhance the forcefulness of the rough language through which he expressed himself and to accentuate the singular effectiveness of his powerful art on the border of restraint and bareness. Since he invariably handled objects and scenes drawn from the most humble existences, everything coalesced to reassure the spectator, to comfort him by giving an impression of balance and serenity as everyday lives unfolded and ran their course, even during the worst moments in modern history. Everything harmoniously invited each viewer to go to the heart of things, to rediscover elementary verities, to feel once more the weight of ordinary things, to be aware of today's means of communication.

The difference between Léger and the Mexican muralists, to whom he generally felt closely akin, was that he persuaded and convinced without resorting to historical senti-

Bathers, 1955
Ink drawing   10 5/8" × 19 5/8" (27 × 50 cm) Louise Leiris Gallery, Paris

mental or imaginative discourse and, as a result, allied himself with the noblest Byzantine or Romanesque tradition, which knew how to achieve eloquence by evoking the most moving simplicity. Using the same methods, as he demonstrated conclusively in a number of ballet sets and illustrations, with his schematic forms, his syncopated rhythms, his authoritative Purism, he reincarnated the very spirit of primitive art. Unlike those who laboriously sought to be inspired by Negro sculpture, he unwittingly achieved the immediate fusion and the successful and lofty synthesis of very distant and different cultures. Finally, through his need to comprehend reality, his desire to make something objective and permanent in the manner of the great classics, the candor of expression in his paintings and his unflagging concern with the human condition, he inevitably arrived at the universality that distinguishes his talent.

By his habitual generosity, his uninterrupted teaching, he proved that he was up to the task of creating around him a climate of understanding and of winning the approval and enthusiasm of those who followed him. He enabled his many students, who came from the four corners of the earth, to make an inventory of the needs of the age and to demonstrate their talent brilliantly later on. It can also be argued that he helped to change the face of cities almost everywhere. In this respect, he was perhaps the only great master of contemporary art who acted as an example and engaged as much as he could in every area of creative art, thus restoring the artist's place to center stage and assigning to him a major role in the necessary transformation of society.

To appreciate the immense and profound impression he left behind him, it is sufficient to cite most of the contemporary painters and the principal movements of the time: from the Abstractionists to the Kineticists, from the neo-Realists, who used industrial objects

Face with Flower, 1930. Drawing   12 5/8" × 9 7/8" (32 × 25 cm)

THREE WOMEN ON RED BACKGROUND, 1927. Oil on canvas   54 3/4″ × 37 3/4″ (139 × 96 cm)
Private collection

to rehabilitate the whole field of narrative representations, to the super-Realists and those who were enchanted by the tonic virtues of color. It is impossible to estimate how much is owed to him, perhaps indirectly, for he shaped the face of our century and determined the direction it will take in the future, heralding the course of things to come.

That is why it is essential to recall Léger's virtues and the success he achieved after such an unrelenting struggle, and also, as Jean Bazaine wrote in 1942, "the steps on the way to grandeur. . . the courage with which he renewed his efforts. . . the great tradition of lyrical expression." Is it not now time—more than time—for all of us to acknowledge our debt of common gratitude, to which Léger is so unquestionably entitled?

GASTON DIEHL

The Studio of Today. The sixth person from left to right: Franciska Clausen.
The first pupil: Otto Carlsund. 1924. Photograph

Exhibition F. Léger and
His Scandinavian Pupils
at Watteau House.
On the left: Erik Olson,
Franciska Clausen.
On the right: Otto Carlsund
1924 Photograph

THE GREAT PARADE, 1954
Oil on canvas   117 3/4″ × 157 1/2″ (299 × 400 cm)
The Solomon R. Guggenheim Museum, New York

The Accordeonist, 1932
Drawing   25 5/8″ × 19 5/8″ (65 × 50 cm)
Charles Kriwin Gallery, Brussels

BIOGRAPHY

1881 Born February 4 in Argentan, France; his father, Henri-Armand Léger, a livestock farmer, died a few years later; his mother, Marie-Adèle Daunou, lived on her farm at Lisores until 1922.

1890–96 Pupil at the Argentan school and at a parish school at Tinchebray.

1897–99 With the consent of his uncle, served as an apprentice with a Caen architect.

1900–2 Draftsman for an architect in Paris.

1900–3 Military service as a sapper in the Second Corps of Engineers at Versailles.

1903 Accepted by the Ecole des Arts Décoratifs; rejected by the Beaux-Arts but, as an unregistered pupil, attended the courses of Gérôme and Ferrier informally. Also frequently visited the Julian Academy and the Louvre.

1904–7 A difficult period. Shared a studio with André Mare, also a native of Argentan; worked in an architect's studio and as a retoucher for a photographer. Fell sick in the winter of 1906 and stayed with his friend Viel at Belgodire in Corsica, where he returned on several occasions. Much impressed by the Cézanne retrospective at the Salon des Indépendants of 1907.

1908–9 Settled in La Ruche, where he made the acquaintance of Archipenko, Laurens, and Lipchitz, and later of Soutine, Chagall, Delaunay, and some visitors, such as Max Jacob, Apollinaire, Raynal, and Cendrars. Became friendly with some of them. Exhibited at the Salon d'Automne and met Henri Rousseau.

1910 Kahnweiler, who was already sponsoring Picasso and Braque, bought some of his works. At the home of Jacques Villon in Puteaux he frequently met the group of the Section d'Or.

1911 Took up residence on the Rue de l'Ancienne-Comédie. Together with Gleizes, Delaunay, and others, he exhibited his *Nudes in the Forest* in Room 41, known as the Cubist Room of the Salon des Indépendants, and also exhibited with them in Brussels. Showed *The Wedding* at the Salon d'Automne.

1912 Exhibited at the Salon des Indépendants with *The Smokers,* at the Salon d'Automne with *Woman in Blue,* and in some other group shows, particularly those of the Section d'Or. Showed at Kahnweiler's.

1913 In May gave a lecture at the Wassiliev Academy, the text of which was reprinted in Paris, Berlin, and Bergen. Participated in the Salon des Indépendants, the Armory Show, and the First Salon d'Automne in Berlin. In October signed a contract with Kahnweiler and took a studio, which he retained until the end of his life, at 86 Rue Notre-Dame-des-Champs.

1914–16 In May delivered another lecture at the Wassiliev Academy. Drafted into the Engineers on August 2, spending two years on the Argonne front. Continued to draw in the trenches and behind the lines. Was a stretcher-bearer at Verdun, where he was gassed in September 1916.

1917 Started painting again during his convalescence in the hospital at Villepinte. Discharged from the army at the end of the year.

1918–19 Intensive work, including illustrations for books by Cendrars; married Jeanne Lohy. Began *Discs, The City,* and *Mechanical Elements.* Exhibited in Paris at Léonce Rosenberg's Galerie de l'Effort Moderne, in Antwerp at the Galerie Sélection.

1920 At the time of the founding of the journal "L'Esprit Nouveau" became friendly with Le Corbusier. Produced *The Mechanic* and *Three Women.* For several years exhibited at the Salon des Indépendants.

1921 Worked with Cendrars on Abel Gance's film "The Wheel"; illustrated Malraux's "Paper Moons"; met Van Doesburg and Mondrian.

1922 Did sets, costumes, and curtain for "Skating Rink," with music by Darius Milhaud, given by the Swedish Ballet of Rolf de Maré.

1923 Again for Rolf de Maré, designed the sets and costumes for "The Creation of the World," with a book by Cendrars and music by Milhaud. Helped with the sets for Marcel Herbier's film "L'Inhumaine" with music by Milhaud; at the Salon des Indépendants, worked on the design of a hall.

1924 Made the film "Ballet Mécanique," with photographs by Man Ray and Dudley Murphy and music by G. Antheil; set up a studio open to the general public with Ozenfant, Marie Laurencin, and Exter. Gave a lecture at the Sorbonne. Traveled in Italy with Rosenberg and fell in love with Ravenna.

1925–27 Had some abstract decorative panels accepted at the Exposition des Arts Décoratifs for the L'Esprit Nouveau pavilion built by Le Corbusier and the pavilion of the French Embassy designed by Mallet-Stevens. Exhibited in New York at the Anderson Galleries and the following year at the Brooklyn Museum; in Paris at the Galerie de Quatre-Chemins, and had a retrospective at the Salon des Indépendants. His attention focused increasingly on objects.

1928 Showed 100 collected works at the Flechtheim Gallery in Berlin and gave a lecture; exhibited in Paris at the Galerie de l'Effort Moderne.

1929 Opened the Académie Moderne with Ozenfant.

1930 Exhibited in London at the Leicester Galleries and in Paris at the Galerie Paul Rosenberg. Became friendly with Calder.

1931 During the summer stayed with his friends the Murphys in Austria; between September and December traveled to New York and Chicago, where he exhibited at the John Becker Gallery and the Durand-Ruel Galleries.

1932 Taught at the Grande Chaumière; traveled in Scandinavia; exhibited at the Valentine Gallery in New York.

1933 Attended large exhibition at the Kunsthaus in Zurich;

went to Greece with Le Corbusier for a convention of the C.I.A.M. On the return boat trip, gave a lecture on "Architecture Confronts Life."

1934 Exhibited at the Galerie Vignon; during the summer stayed with the Murphys in Antibes; in August traveled to London to work on the sets of an H. G. Wells film, "The Shape of Things to Come"; in September went to Stockholm for his exhibition at the Modern Gallery. Gave a lecture at the Sorbonne, "From the Acropolis to the Eiffel Tower."

1935 Traveled to Brussels for the World Exhibition, for which he did a mural decoration for a sports pavilion to be built by Charlotte Perriand. In September returned to the United States, where Le Corbusier joined him to attend an impressive exhibition at the Museum of Modern Art in New York, then at the Art Institute in Chicago.

1936 Demonstrated the independence of his thinking in a debate on "The Argument Against Realism"; for a year was active in the Salon d'Art Mural.

1937 Made sets for "David Triumphant," a ballet for the Paris Opera House by Serge Lifar with music by Riéti; did the décor for a trade union festival at the Vélodrome d'Hiver and a mural at the Palais de la Découverte for the World Exhibition which had rejected several of his projects. In November gave a lecture in Antwerp on "Color in the World." Traveled to Helsinki for his exhibition at the Artek Gallery; became friendly with Aalto.

1938–39 Spent the summer in Vézelay with Le Corbusier. From September to March he was in the United States, where he decorated the apartment of Nelson A. Rockefeller and gave a series of eight lectures on "Color in Architecture" at Yale University. In Paris, produced the sets for "Birth of a City," a play by J. B. Bloch performed at the Vélodrome d'Hiver.

1940–41 Managed to reach Bordeaux from Lisores, and from there Marseilles, where in late October he succeeded in boarding a ship bound for the United States. Taught at Yale, together with Focillon, Milhaud, and Maurois. Showed his *Composition with Two Parrots* at the Museum of Modern Art, New York. During the summer conducted a course at Mills College, where he organized an exhibition. Began *The Divers*.

1942–45 Exhibited at the gallery of Paul Rosenberg; met other exiled artists at Pierre Matisse's and became friendly with R. P. Couturier. Produced for a film by Hans Richter the sequence "The Girl with the Manufactured Heart." Exhibited at the Fogg Art Museum in Cambridge, the Valentine Gallery, the Samuel Kootz Gallery in New York, and the Galerie Louis Carré in Paris. Returned to France in December 1945.

1946–47 R. P. Couturier asked him to do a mosaic for the façade of a church in Plateau d'Assy, to be completed in 1949. Gave a lecture at the Sorbonne on "Work and Culture" and held an exhibition at the Galerie Louis Carré. Spent the summer of 1947 in Normandy.

1948 Made sets for "The Steel Step" with music by Prokofiev, for the Ballet des Champs-Elysées. Together with his pupils, did the décor for the International Congress of Women at the Porte de Versailles. In June, at the School of the Louvre, presided with Diehl at the founding of the "International Federation of Films on Art" and at the first festival organized around this theme. Went to Poland for the Peace Congress in Wrocław. Took part, with Bazaine and Diehl, in a debate on "The Art of Today" for "The Friends of Art" in Brussels and Antwerp.

1949 Retrospective at the Musée National d'Art Moderne in Paris; text and illustrations for "The Circus," published by Tériade; illustrations for "The Illuminations" by Rimbaud; set and costumes for the opera "Bolivar" by Darius Milhaud. Produced his first ceramics with Roland Brice in Biot.

1950 Finished *The Builders*. Exhibited at the Tate Gallery in London. Made a mosaic for the crypt of the American Memorial in Bastogne. Erected a ceramics studio in Biot. Attended the dedication of the church of Plateau d'Assy.

1951 Introduced the first polychrome sculptures at the Galerie Leiris. Went to Milan, where he produced a large composition for the Triennale. In September, installed seventeen stained-glass windows and a tapestry in the church of Audincourt. Stayed in Chevreuse during an attack of sciatica.

1952 In February married Nadia Khodossevich, who had entered the Academy in 1924 as a pupil and then became an assistant. Settled at Gros Tilleul in Gif-sur-Yvette. In April delivered a lecture in Berne on the occasion of his exhibition at the Kunsthalle. Exhibited at the Antibes Museum, the Galerie Berri, the Galerie Louis Carré in Paris, and the Sidney Janis Gallery in New York. Traveled to Venice to attend the twenty-sixth Biennale. Produced panels for the great assembly hall of the United Nations in New York. Did sets and costumes for a ballet by Janine Charrat at Amboise.

1953 Had a traveling exhibition in Japan. Exhibited at the Museum of Modern Art in New York, then at the Art Institute of Chicago and in San Francisco. Showed his polychrome sculptures at the Galerie Louis Carré. Lectured in Brussels on "Modern Painting." Did illustrations for the poem "Liberty" by Eluard.

1954 Produced mosaic and stained-glass windows for the University of Caracas ordered by Raul Villanueva, stained-glass windows in Caracas for Innocente Palacios, and for the church of Courfaivre. Did preliminary studies for the Memorial Hospital in Saint-Lô to be opened in 1956. Showed *The Picnic* and *The Great Parade* at the Maison de la Pensée Française.

1955 Produced first sketches of *The Battle of Stalingrad*. Went to Prague for the Sokols Congress. Completed a mural for Gaz de France at Alfortville. First prize at the São Paulo Biennale. Retrospective at the Museum of Lyons. Died on August 17 at Gif-sur-Yvette. Maeght Gallery staged "Tribute to Fernand Léger."

1982 Nadia Léger dies.

CONCISE BIBLIOGRAPHY

A complete bibliography appeared in the book by Douglas Cooper (1949), in the catalogue of the Palais des Beaux-Arts of Brussels (1956), in the catalogue of the Museum of Modern Art in New York (1962), and a selective one in the catalogue of the Grand Palais, Paris (1972).

ARTICLES BY FERNAND LÉGER

The most important of numerous writings by the author and the texts of interviews that he gave have been collected in:

LÉGER, Fernand: *Propos et présence*. Paris: Gonthier-Séghers, 1959.

LÉGER, Fernand: *Fonctions de la peinture*. Paris: Gonthier, 1965; Berne: Bentelli, 1971; New York: Viking, 1973; London: Thames and Hudson, 1973.

GARAUDY, Roger: *Pour un réalisme du XXᵉ siècle*. Paris: Grasset, 1968.

MONOGRAPHS

RAYNAL, Maurice: *Fernand Léger*. Paris: L'Effort Moderne, 1920.

TÉRIADE, E.: *Fernand Léger*. Paris: Cahiers d'Art, 1928.

GEORGE, Waldemar: *Fernand Léger*. Paris: Gallimard, 1929.

ELGAR, Franck: *Léger, peintures 1911–1948*. Paris: Ed. du Chêne, 1948.

MONTALTE, Louis: *La Basilique universelle de la paix et du pardon (La Sainte-Baume)*. Levallois-Perret, 1948.

COOPER, Douglas: *Fernand Léger et le nouvel espace*. Geneva: Les Trois Collines, 1949.

ROY, Claude: *Fernand Léger, Les constructeurs*. Paris: La Falaise, 1951.

ZERVOS, Christian: *Fernand Léger, œuvres de 1905 à 1952*. Paris: Cahiers d'Art, 1952.

MAUROIS, André: *Mon ami Léger*. Paris: Louis Carré, 1952.

JARDOT, Maurice: *Léger, dessins*. Paris: Les Deux Mondes, 1953.

Men with Truck, 1935
Ink drawing   17 3/4" × 22 7/8" (45 × 58 cm) Louise Leiris Gallery, Paris

KUH, Katherine: *Léger*. Urbana: University of Illinois Press, 1953.

ELGAR, Franck: *Picasso et Léger*. Paris: Les Amis de l'Art, 1954.

Entretiens de Fernand Léger avec Blaise Cendrars et Louis Carré sur le paysage. Paris: Louis Carré, 1954.

DESCARGUES, Pierre: *Fernand Léger, le dynamisme pictural*. Geneva: Pierre Cailler, 1955.

VERDET, André: *Fernand Léger*. Geneva: Kister, 1956.

JARDOT, Maurice: *Fernand Léger*. Paris: Hazan, 1956.

PARMELIN, Hélène: *Cinq peintres et le théâtre*. Paris: Cercle d'Art, 1956.

VALLIER, Dora: *Léger, carnet*. Paris, Cahiers d'Art, 1958.

ARAGON, Louis: *Fernand Léger, contrastes*. Paris: Au Vent d'Arles, 1959.

DELEVOY, Robert: *F. Léger*. Geneva: Skira, 1962.

TADINI, Emilio: *Fernand Léger*. Milan: Fratelli Fabbri, 1964; Paris: Hachette, 1967.

PETROVA, Eva: *Fernand Léger*. Prague: Orbis, 1966.

LIGOCKI, Alfred: *Trzy spotkania ze światem widzialnym: Picasso, Matisse, Léger*. Warsaw: Wiedza Powszechna, 1967.

DÉROUDILLE, René: *Léger*. Paris: Bordas, 1968.

GARAUDY, Roger: *Pour un réalisme du XXe siècle: dialogue posthume avec Fernand Léger*. Paris: Grasset, 1968.

FRANCIA, Peter de: *Léger's "The Great Parade"*. London: Cassel, 1969

BLONDEL, Elisabeth: *Fernand Léger et les arts du spectacle*. Paris: Unpublished doctoral dissertation, 1969.

DE SMET, Chantal: *Fernand Léger, sociaal idealistisch kunstenaar*. Ghent: Unpublished doctoral dissertation

DANE, Marie Claude: *Fernand Léger*. Paris: Musée Galliéra, 1969.

VERDET, André: *Fernand Léger* (text in Italian and French), Florence: Sadea Sansoni, 1969.

WILLIAM, Charles: *A Comparative Study of the Views of Present Reality Manifested in the Art Works of Fernand Léger and Edgar Varèse*. Athens: Unpublished doctoral dissertation, Ohio University, 1970.

ZADOVA, L.: *Fernand Léger (mosaique, vitrail, céramique, tapisserie)*. Moscow: Iskusstvo, 1970.

GARAUDY, Roger: *Esthétique et invention du futur*. Paris: Union Générale d'Editions, 1971.

LE NOCI, Guido: *Fernand Léger*. Milan. Apollinaire, 1971.

DEAC, Mircea: *Léger*. Bucharest; Meridiane, 1972.

CASSOU, Jean and LEYMARIE, Jean: *Léger, dessins et gouaches*. Paris: Ed. du Chêne, 1972; London: Thames and Hudson, 1973.

GREEN, C.: *Fernand Léger and the Parisian "Avant-garde," 1909–1921*. London: Unpublished doctoral dissertation, Courtauld Institute of Art, 1973.

GREEN, C.: *Léger and the Avant Garde*. New Haven: Yale University Press, 1976.

SCHMALENBACH W.: *Léger*. Cologne: DuMont, 1977; Paris: Cercle d'Art, 1977.

VERDET, A.: *Entretiens, notes et écrits sur la peinture, Braque, Léger, Matisse, Picasso*. Paris: Galilée, 1978.

F. Léger, la poésie de l'objet 1928–34. Paris: Cabinet des dessins, Centre Georges Pompidou, Musée National d'Art Moderne, 1981.

F. Léger, Gouaches et dessins 1911–1955. Paris: Galerie Louise Leiris, 1981.

Hommage à Fernand Léger (1881–1955), Exposition du Centenaire, Musée National Fernand Léger, Biot, France. Le Petit Journal des Grandes Expositions, 1981.

LAUGIER, Cl. et RICHET, Michèle: *Œuvres de Fernand Léger*. Paris: Collections du Musée National d'Art Moderne, 1981.

ARTICLES PUBLISHED IN PERIODICALS SINCE 1970

"Fernand Léger und die engagierte Kunst." *Kunstnachrichten*, Switzerland, 6 (1969–70), pp. 3–13.

PFEIFFER, G.: "Ausstellung Fernand Léger in Düsseldorf." *Kunstwerk*, Stuttgart, No. 23 (1970), p. 80.

STABER, M.: "Fernand Léger in Düsseldorf". *Art International*, Lugano, March 1970, p. 58.

GOLDING, J.: "Léger, Waddington Galleries London exhibition." *Studio*, No. 179 (1970), pp. 226–27.

LOGINOV, V.: "U frantsuskikh khudozhnikov." *Iskusstvo*, Moscow, 33 (1970), pp. 51–59.

PETRIA, B.: "Léger at the Waddington Galleries." *The Burlington Magazine*, London, June 1970, p. 409.

SACKS, Lois: "Fernand Léger and the Ballets Suédois." *Apollo*, No. 91 (1970), pp. 463–68.

"Léger's The Mechanic, National Gallery of Canada." *The Burlington Magazine*, London, July 1970, p. 448.

"Exhibition at Blue Moon Gallery." *Art News*, New York, summer 1970, p. 68.

"Léger, Contre Le Corbusier Ausstellung." *Werk*, Winterthur, August 1970, p. 556.

GALLEGO: "Léger otra vez." *Goya*, Madrid, No. 98 (1970), p. 100.

SPIELMANN, H.: "Léger im Muscum für Kunst, Hamburg." *Jahr. Hamburger Kunstsamml*. No. 14–15 (1970), pp. 410–13.

LORDS, B.: "Léger in the Galleries of Montreal." *Arts Canada*, No. 27 (1970), p. 86.

APPLEGATE, J.: "Léger, Maeght Paris exhibition." *Art International*, Lugano, November 1970, pp. 83–84.

BANHAM, R.: "Nature Morte Lives." *New Society*, November 26, 1970, pp. 958–59.

"Léger, Galerie Beyeler, Basel." *Werk*, November 1970, p. 799.

DUNLOP, I.: "Léger, Tate Gallery Exhibition." *Apollo*, No. 92 (1970), pp. 382–83.

DESCARGUES, Pierre: "Fernand Léger et la règle des contrastes." *XXe siècle*, No. 33 (1970), pp. 38–47.

"Kirchenfenster im Jura." *Schweiz*, No. 11 (1970), p. 11.

GREEN, C.: "Léger, Purism." *Art News*, New York, December 1970, pp. 54–56.

BLUNT, A.: "Léger at the Tate." *Listener*, 3 December 1970, pp. 792–93.

BURN, G.: "Léger and Purist Paris, Tate Gallery." *Arts Review*, No. 24 (1970), pp. 788–89.

CABANNE, Pierre: "Le purisme ou la recherche de l'absolu." *Jardin des Arts*, December 1970, pp. 44–51.

CAUSEY, A.: "Léger and Purist Paris." *Illustrated London News*, December 12, 1970, p. 21.

DENVIR, B.: "Léger, Tate Gallery Exhibition." *Art International*, Lugano, January 1971. pp. 15–22.

"Poussin of Pigalle." *Art and Artists*, London, January 1971, pp. 16–19.

WADLEY, N.: "Léger and Purist Paris." *The Burlington Magazine*, London, January 1971, pp. 55–56.

BENTHALL, J.: "Léger's City and Atget's." *Studio*, No. 181 (1971), pp. 7–8.

FORGE, A.: "Forces Against Object-Based Art." *Studio*, No. 181 (1971), p. 36.

PLEYNET, M.: "Léger, Galerie Claude Bernard." *Art International*, Lugano, February 1971, p. 50.

VAIZEY, M.: "Léger, Tate Gallery Exhibition." *Connoisseur*, February 1971, p. 150.

KRAMER, M.: "Cubist Epoch." *Art in America*, March 1971, p. 56.

KENNEDY, R. C.: "Léger, Galerie Claude Bernard." *Art International*, Lugano, April 1971, pp. 34–35.

"Cubist Epoch at the Metropolitan." *Arts* 20 (1971), p. 53.

MARUSSI, Garibaldo: "Apoteosi di Léger." *Arti* 20 (1971), pp. 2 7.

RICHET, Michèle: "Fernand Léger aux Galeries Nationales." *Revue du Louvre et des Musées de France* 21 (1971), pp. 311–13.

METKEN, Günter: "Das geplante Paradies, Léger-Retrospektive in Paris." *Weltkunst* 41 (1971), pp. 1517–18.

GRAFF, Piotr: "Spełnione i niespełnione funkcje malarstwa." *Mies. Lit.*, Warsaw, 6 (1971), pp. 138–40.

PELLATON, Jean-Paul: "Les Vitraux." *Alliance culturelle romande*, No. 17 (1971), pp. 144–46.

"Fernand Léger," *Chroniques de l'art vivant*. October 1971, pp. 14–15.

BEAUVAIS DE: "Fernand Léger." *Paris-Match*, October 23, 1971, pp. 50–59.

ANDERS, Henryk: "Droga Légera." *Prz. art.*, Warsaw, No. 5 (1971), pp. 13–21.

FRANCIA, J. A. and FRIGERIO, S.: "Léger ou Bacon." *Coloquio Artes*, Lisbon, 14 (1972), pp. 4–9.

"Léger, Grand Palais Exhibition." *Art News*, New York, February 1972, p. 22.

"Léger, Pace Gallery, New York Exhibition." *Art News*, New York, March 1972, p. 18.

"Fernand Léger, le peuple du monde mécanique." *Jardin des Arts*, No. 209 (1972), pp. 60–64.

KRAUSS, R.: "Léger, Le Corbusier and Purism." *Artforum*, Iowa, 10 (1972), pp. 50–53.

ELDERFIELD, J.: "Epic Cubism and the Manufactured Object." *Artforum*, Iowa, 10 (1972), pp. 54–63.

WEELEN, Guy: "The Industrial Age and the City." *Vie des Arts*, Montreal, No. 66 (1972), pp. 32–35, 84–86.

WISSER, M.: "Fernand Léger." *Museumjournaal*, Netherlands, 17 (1972), pp. 59–64.

RUSSELL, J.: "Léger, the Master of the Machine." *Horizon*, United States, 14 (1972), pp. 86–95.

GALLEGO, J.: "Léger en perspectiva." *Bellas Artes*, Madrid, No. 14 (1972), pp. 26–28.

RONDOLINO, G.: "Pittori e nomini di cinema, Picabia e Léger." *Ars*, Italy, No. 14 (1973), pp. 66–67, 68–81.

SACKS, L.: "Fernand Léger. The Work of two Decades," *Art and Articles*, pp. 122–131. *Mél. Martieussen* ZA 1973.

"Le rêve de Léger conquiert la terre." *Galerie-Jardin des Arts*, Paris, No. 162 (1976).

ROSENTHAL, J.: "A Recently Discovered Portrait of Leo Stein by Fernand Léger." *Apollo* 104, 65 (1976), pp. 106–7.

JACKIEWICZ, A.: "Pęk kluczy w dziele Légera" (Keys in the Work of Fernand Léger). *Roczn. Hist. Sztuki* 11 (1976), pp. 119–138.

FRANZKE, A.: "Fernand Léger. Fumées sur les toits. Zu einer Neuerwerbung der Staatlichen Kunsthalle, Karlsruhe." *Jb. Staatl. Kunstsammlung Baden-Württ.* 15, 1978, pp. 75–93.

RICHTER, H.: "Der Mensch als Mass. Fernand Légers figürliches Werk in der Kunsthalle Köln." *Weltkunst*, 48. No. 11 (1978), pp. 1308–9.

SCHLUMBERGER, E.: "La parole est aux visages." *Connaissance des Arts*, No 319. Sept. 78.

"Exp. L. Château de Vascœuil." *Connaissance des Arts*, No. 329, July 79.

SPECIAL ISSUES OF PERIODICALS HONORING THE ARTIST

"Fernand Léger." *Sélection*, Antwerp, 8 (1929).

"Exposition Fernand Léger au Kunsthaus de Zurich." *Cahiers d'art* 8 (1933), with Apollinaire, J. Bazin, L. J. Bulliet, B. Cendrars, P. Courthion, I. Ehrenbourg, P. Fierens, W. George, S. Giedion, Heilmeier, R. Hoppe, H. Laugier, Le Corbusier, F. Léger, and others.

Fernand Léger: la forme humaine dans l'espace. Text by M. A. Couturier, S. Giedion, F. Hertel, S. M. Kootz, Fernand Léger, and others, Montreal: l'Arbre, 1945.

"Hommage à Fernand Léger," *Les Lettres Françaises*, Paris, No. 582 (1955), pp. 25–31.

Hommage à Fernand Léger dans le XXe siècle. Text by D. H. Kahnweiler, G. Habasque, J. Cassou, F. Elgar, Nadia Léger, G. Lascault, J. J. Lévêque, A. B. Nakov, P. Waldberg, J. Lassaigne, R. Cogniat, D. Milhaud, J. L. Ferrier, P. Descargues, Y. Taillandier, A. Verdet, H. Galy-Carles, M. Jardot, Paris, 1971.

"Fernand Léger." *Europe*, with Bouvier-Ajam, Descargues, Markovits, Tenand, and others, Paris, No. 508–9 (1971).

"F. Léger." *XXe siècle*. Paris, 1971.

EXHIBITIONS AND CATALOGUES

1933 FERNAND Léger. Zurich: Kunsthaus.

1936 HERRIOT, Edouard: *Modern French Tapestries by Braque, Dufy, Léger, Lurçat, Matisse, Picasso, Rouault*. New York: Bignon Gallery.

1945 BAZAINE, Jean: *Fernand Léger, peintures antérieures à 1940*. Paris: Galerie Louis Carré.

1946 *Fernand Léger, œuvres 1940–1945*. Paris: Galerie Louis Carré.

1947 *Calder, Léger*. Amsterdam: Stedelijk Museum.

1949 *Léger, 1905–1949*. Paris: Musée National d'Art Moderne.

1950 *Léger*. London: The Tate Gallery.

1952 *Fernand Léger*. Berne: Kunsthalle.

1953 KUH, Katherine: *Léger*. New York: Museum of Modern Art. San Francisco Museum; Chicago: The Art Institute.

1954 HUYSMANS, Georges: *Léger, 1953–1954*. Paris: Maison de la Pensée Française.

1955 JULIAN, René: *Léger*. Lyons: Musée des Beaux-Arts.

1956 COOPER, Douglas: *Fernand Léger, dessins de guerre* (War Drawings). Paris: Galerie Berggruen.

1956 CASSOU, Jean: *Fernand Léger*. Brussels: Palais des Beaux-Arts.

1956 MATHEY, François: *Fernand Léger*. Tournon, Paris: Musée des Arts Décoratifs.

1957 *Léger. Major Themes*. New York: Sidney Janis Gallery.

1958 JARDOT, Maurice: *F. Léger, dessins et gouaches*. Paris: Galerie Louise Leiris.

1959 BENESCH, Otto: *Léger, Drucke, Gouachen, Lithographien*. Vienna: Albertina.

1961 *Paintings by Fernand Léger Selected from the Years 1918–1954*. New York: Sidney Janis Gallery.

1962 MESSER, Thomas M.: *Fernand Léger*. New York: The Solomon R. Guggenheim Museum.

1962 COOPER, Douglas: *Fernand Léger. Contrastes de formes 1913–1915*. Paris: Galerie Berggruen.

1963 *Léger*. Moscow.

1964 HULTEN, K. G.: *Fernand Léger*. Stockholm: Moderna Museet.

1965 *La peinture sous le signe de Blaise Cendrars: Delaunay, Léger*. Paris: Galerie Louise Leiris.

1966 COOPER, Douglas: *Fernand Léger*. Marseilles: Musée Cantini.

1967 GAMZU, Haim: *Léger*. Tel-Aviv: Museum of Art.

1968 *Fernand Léger*. Vienna: Rosenbaum.

1968 *Fernand Léger. Oil Paintings*. New York: Perls Galleries.

1968 HUGUES, Patrice: *F. Léger*. Le Havre: Nouveau Musée.

1969 *Léger*. Basel: Galerie Beyeler.

1969 *Léger*. Biot, France: Musée National Fernand Léger.

1969 DANE, Marie-Claude: *Fernand Léger*. Paris: Musée Galliéra.

1969 *Léger*. Düsseldorf: Städtische Kunsthalle.

1969 *Léger and The Machine*. Honolulu: Academy of Arts.

1970 *Léger*. Paris: Galerie Claude Bernard.

1971 *Léger and Purist Paris*. London: The Tate Gallery.

1971 LEYMARIE, Jean: *Léger*. Paris: Grand Palais. Réunion des Musées Nationaux.

1971 *Léger, Picasso: Oelbilder, Gouachen, Wandteppiche*. Cologne: Baukunst.

1975 *F. Léger*. Catalogue with a poem by Blaise Cendrars. Paris: Galerie Berggruen.

1975 *Léger, peintures, gouaches.* Brussels: Galerie Isy Brachot.
1979 *Léger. Gouaches, aquarelles et dessins.* Paris: Galerie Berggruen.
1981 *Fernand Léger, la poésie de l'objet.* Paris: Musée National d'Art Moderne. Centre Georges Pompidou.
1982 FABRE, Gladys C. and BRIOT, Marie Odile: *Fernand Léger et l'esprit moderne—Léger and the Modern Spirit (1918–1931).* Paris: Musée d'Art Moderne de la Ville de Paris; (Mareh June, 1982); Houston: Museum of Fine Arts; Geneva: Musée Rath.
1982 DIEHL, Gaston and SALVADOR, José Maria: *Fernand Léger 1905–1955.* Caracas: Museo de Arte Contemporáneo.

BOOKS ILLUSTRATED BY THE ARTIST

CENDRARS, Blaise: *J'ai tué,* 5 drawings. Paris: La Belle Edition, 1918. Paris: Georges Crès, 1919; Woodstock, New York: The Plowshare, 1919.

CENDRARS, Blaise: *La Fin du Monde, filmée par l'Ange Notre Dame,* 20 ill. in color. Paris: La Sirène, 1919.

GOLL, Ivan: *Die Chapliniade,* 4 drawings. Dresden: Kaemmerer Verlag, Berlin, 1920.

MALRAUX, André: *Lunes en papier,* 6 woodcuts. Paris: Galerie Simon, 1921.

GOLL, Ivan: *Le Nouvel Orphée.* Ill. by several artists including Léger. Paris: La Sirène, 1923.

GANZO, Robert: *Orénoque,* 3 drawings. Paris: 1937.

GUILLEVIC: *Coordonnées,* 20 drawings. Geneva, Paris: Les Trois Collines, 1948.

MASSON, Loys: *L'Illustre Thomas Wilson.* 6 drawings and 1 lithograph. Paris: Bordas, 1948.

RIMBAUD, Arthur: *Les Illuminations,* 15 lithographs. Lausanne: Louis Groschlaude, 1949.

LÉGER, Fernand: *Le Cirque,* text by the artist, 60 lithographs. Paris: Tériade, 1949.

LÉGER, Fernand: In *Derrière le Miroir,* 2 lithographs. Paris: Galerie Maeght, May 1949.

ÉLUARD, Paul: *Liberté.* Paris, 1953.

TZARA, Tristan: *La Face intérieure.* 1 lithograph. Paris: P. Seghers. 1953.

LÉGER, Fernand: *La Ville.* 29 lithographs. Paris: Tériade, 1959.

LÉGER, Fernand: *Mes Voyages,* with a poem by Aragon, 28 lithographs. Paris: Editeurs Français Réunis, 1960.

VERDET, André: *Songe de Fernand Léger,* several drawings. Paris: Georges Israel, 1976.